D0007586

Mexico's Foreign Trade and Economic Development

Published in cooperation with
the University of Michigan Graduate
Research Seminar in International Economics

PRAEGER SPECIAL STUDIES IN
INTERNATIONAL ECONOMICS AND DEVELOPMENT

Mexico's Foreign Trade and Economic Development

William O. Freithaler

FREDERICK A. PRAEGER, Publishers
New York · Washington · London

The purpose of the Praeger Special Studies is to make specialized research monographs in U.S. and international economics and politics available to the academic, business, and government communities. For further information, write to the Special Projects Division, Frederick A. Praeger, Publishers, 111 Fourth Avenue, New York, N.Y. 10003.

FREDERICK A. PRAEGER, PUBLISHERS
111 Fourth Avenue, New York, N.Y. 10003, U.S.A.
77-79 Charlotte Street, London W.1, England

Published in the United States of America in 1968
by Frederick A. Praeger, Inc., Publishers

Library of Congress Catalog Card Number: 67-22281

Printed in the United States of America

PREFACE

Since World War II, many economists have come to regard external economic difficulties as one of the most intractable constraints limiting the growth achievements of the less-developed nations. Nonetheless, a number of relatively poor countries that are deeply involved in international commerce have, in fact, managed to generate sustained and impressive growth performances over the past two or three decades. The developmental achievements of Mexico--along with those of such countries as Brazil, Israel, Italy, Japan, Venezuela, and Yugoslavia--are particularly interesting in this respect.

The primary purpose of this study is to analyze Mexico's attempt to come to grips with its changing external economic environment since 1940. The economic adjustments made to cope with the nation's trade problems are also viewed in terms of their relation to certain major socio-economic difficulties that Mexico has thus far failed to solve. The latter include the much-discussed income distribution question and the closely related issue of regional biases in the national pattern of economic development.

The reader will, of course, find no panacea in this volume for the trade problems of the many poor countries whose situation may be similar to that faced by Mexico during these early stages of its drive toward economic maturity. Nevertheless, in certain relatively modest ways, it is possible that other countries may benefit from Mexico's experience.

I wish to express my thanks to the patrons and administrators of the Foreign Area Fellowship Program for providing a substantial portion of the funds that enabled me to carry out the research in support of this work. I am also indebted to Professors Robin Barlow, Robinson Gregory, Richard Porter, Robert Stern, and Wolfgang Stolper--all of the University of Michigan--for their kind and patient help in reading and criticizing the earlier drafts of this work.

Many other people helped in the tedious process of collecting data, including various staff members of the Banco de México, Nacional Financiera, and the U.S. Department of Commerce. Most of all, however, I owe thanks in this regard to Professor Nettie Lee Benson and her staff at the Garcia Collection in the University of Texas Library.

CONTENTS

LIST OF TABLES AND FIGURES

Table		Page

Table		Page

Figure

LIST OF ORGANIZATIONS AND ABBREVIATIONS

AID	U.S. Agency for International Development
DAC	Development Assistance Committee of the Organization for Economic Cooperation and Development
ECLA	The United Nations Economic Commission for Latin America
FAO	Food and Agriculture Organization of the United Nations
GATT	Contracting Parties of the General Agreement on Tariffs and Trade
GNP	Gross National Product
IADB	Inter-American Development Bank
IBRD	International Bank for Reconstruction and Development
ISA	International Sugar Agreement
NAFIN	Nacional Financiera S.A. (a Mexican Development Bank)
OECD	Organization for Economic Cooperation and Development
PRONAF	Programa Nacional Fronteriza (the Mexican Frontier Development Program)
SITC	Standard International Trade Classification
UN	United Nations
USDA	United States Department of Agriculture

San Diego
TIJUANA
MEXICALI
TUCSON
El Paso
Ciudad Juárez
NOGALES
HERMOSILLO
CHIHUAHUA
Delicias
CIUDAD OBREGON
HILDAGO DEL PARRAL
GOMEZ PALACIO
TORREÓN
CULIACAN
DURANGO
MAZATLÁN
BAJA CALIFORNIA
Gulf of California
La Paz
Ciudad Acuña
Del Rio
Eagle Pass
PIEDRAS NEGRAS
NUEVA ROSITA
Monclova
San Antonio
NUEVO LAREDO
Mc ALLEN
HARLINGEN
BROWNSVILLE
MATAMOROS
REYNOSA
Monterrey
SALTILLO
CIUDAD VICTORIA
TAMPICO
FRESNILLO
ZACATECAS
AQUASCALIENTES
LEON
GUANAJUATO
QUERETARO
PACHUCA
GUADALAJARA
IRAPUATO
MORELIA
MÉXICO
TOLUCA
CUERNAVACA
PUEBLA
CORDOBA
ORIZABA
VERACRUZ
COLIMA
OAXACA
Chilpancingo
ACAPULCO
Isthmus of Tehuantepec
VILLAHERMOSA
CAMPECHE
MÉRIDA
GULF OF MEXICO
MEXICO
-N-
0
100
200
300
Statute miles

CHAPTER 1 INTRODUCTION

This study interprets the role foreign trade has played in the process of economic development in Mexico since 1940. It specifically attempts to determine how Mexico has come to grips with the following much-discussed dilemma facing growth-conscious developing countries:

> In the course of development, the rate of growth of imports tends to be more rapid than the rate of growth of national output, and the demand for imports tends to exceed the export-based capacity to import--especially during the early phases when the increase in investment is sizeable and structural changes are considerable. The poor country then confronts a conflict between accelerating its internal development and maintaining external balance.[1]

Generalized to include all poor countries, or regional groupings of them, the foregoing dilemma forms the basis of what has come to be known as the "trade-gap problem." A number of empirical works by various internal agencies, and a recent comprehensive study by Bela Balassa, examine the various aspects of the problem in considerable detail.[2] Such "trade-gap" studies provide a useful theoretical framework for analyzing Mexico's attempt to come to grips with the external economic problems encountered during the recent era of rapid growth.[3] The Mexican experience in turn serves as an interesting though limited specific test of various propositions and generalizations commonly encountered in "trade-gap" studies.

Nowadays it is virtually impossible to find an individual country's national plan specifying a target growth rate of less than 4 per cent per year. More ambitious targets, on the order of 5 to 8 per cent per year, are usually selected.[4] The practice of framing development plans designed to achieve such goals has been actively encouraged by various international agencies on the grounds that more modest achievements will not suffice to reverse the trend toward growing international income disparities.[5] Failure to reverse such a trend is thought to be fraught with grave dangers of heightened political and social unrest in world affairs.[6] Other development objectives are, of course, also sought; nevertheless, primary emphasis is always on accelerating the over-all growth rate, because it is in the nature of a prerequisite for the realization of most other social goals.

It is not surprising, therefore, to find that most "trade-gap" studies either posit, or at any rate consider, the implications of the 5 per cent minimal growth target specified in the United Nations General Assembly Resolution launching the so-called Decade of Development.[7] Balassa's study is the most ambitious in this respect in that it works out the implications of both this "target" rate and a lower, "most likely," rate of growth.[8]

"Trade-gap" studies then go on to gauge the "irreducible import needs" associated with the desired income streams in the less developed countries.[9] First, an attempt is made to project the need for visible (merchandise) imports. Balassa, for example, disaggregates the underdeveloped world on a regional basis and applies estimated income elasticities of import demand (for merchandise) ranging from a low of .7-.8 (for Latin America) to a high of 1.2 (for the Middle East).[10] He bases these estimates on the recent import experiences of such regions and on anticipated import coefficients cited in development plans of particular countries.[11] The U.N. also uses an average estimated income elasticity of import demand greater than one, based on import/income relationships for the 1950's. These U.N. findings in turn support Raul Prebisch's view of the "irreducible import needs" associated with U.N. growth targets.

> What are the implications of the 5 per cent minimum growth target for international trade? First and foremost it should not be expected that, if the income of all developing countries is to rise at the minimum of 5 per cent every year, their imports can increase at a rate much less than 6 per cent. One of the main reasons for this is that any acceleration in the rate of growth requires additional investment; and the import content of this investment is normally much higher than that of income as a whole.[12] [Emphasis added.]

Armed, then, with such import coefficients, "trade-gap" studies simply apply them to future income streams to determine the visible (merchandise) import needs connected with given growth rates. To this, they add projections of the need for the (invisible) services of foreigners; that is, transport services, investment income payments, and so on. Thus projected, rapid rises in "import needs" provide the basic source of pressure on the export sectors of the developing economies, since much of the needed exchange must be earned via an increased volume of exports, possibly in the face of adverse movements in the terms of trade.[13]

Attention is then focused on the issue of whether or not the export bases of the developing countries can be expected to provide the needed exchange. As in the case of imports, various techniques have been used to project the export earnings likely to accrue to the developing countries as a group. The method commonly used by U.N. agencies essentially involves applying the advanced countries' combined historical propensity to import from the developing countries to the "most likely" future income stream in the advanced countries.[14] This rather simplified approach stands in marked contrast to the exhaustive market-by-market commodity type of analysis pursued, for example, by Bela Balassa.[15]

Regardless of the methods, however, the basic results are the same in kind, though not in degree, in all "trade-gap" studies. That is to say, the less-developed countries, as a group, are certain to face a large "trade-gap" on current account of their composite balance of payments if they attempt to grow at the ambitious "target" rate discussed above. Samples of the projected magnitudes of the aforementioned deficits for 1970 are, respectively, $20, $12, and $13-20 billion (U.S.) in the findings of the U.N. Secretariat,[16] Bela Balassa,[17] and the Bellagio Conference.[18].

Such hypothetical current account deficits consist of two major elements. The first and largest of these is the anticipated merchandise import surplus, accounting, for example, for $11 of the $20 billion in the trade gap as calculated by the U.N., and $6.8 of the $12 billion in the Balassa study. Substantial anticipated deficits under the current account invisible (service) headings account for the remaining portions of the "trade-gaps."[19]

These hypothetical gaps could conceivably be offset via roughly equal net long-term capital flows toward the less developed countries.[20] By 1970, this method of resolving the problem would seemingly require that somewhere between two-sevenths[21] and two-fifths[22] of the "irreducible import needs" of the poor countries be financed via capital flows. The interesting question that arises is: Are capital flows in fact likely to be large enough to offset the projected gaps? Assuming "target" growth achievement in the poor countries, and "most likely" values for other key variables, "trade-gap" studies invariably answer in the negative. For example, Balassa, whose key assumptions are far less pessimistic than those made in the U.N. studies, reaches just such a conclusion, though he states what is sought in the poor countries as the "exception":

> It has been shown that the current account deficit of the developing countries, taken together, could be financed by the projected inflow of foreign capital, excepting the case that national income grew in these countries at target rates and developed economies attained 'most likely' growth rates.[23]

The U.N. Secretariat's calculation for the hypothetical 1970 "residual trade-gap" (net of anticipated capital inflows) amounts to a remarkable $11 billion (U.S.) at 1960 prices.[24] Part of this may be due to the U.N.'s tendency to "adjust" their empirical findings to emphasize the urgency of the problem at hand. For example, consider the following note in the technical appendix to the study by the U.N. Secretariat:

> In order to avoid gross underestimation of the import requirements, a *conjectural* figure has been added to the hypothetical level of imports of each region derived from the above [regression] equations.[25] [Emphasis added.]

It would appear, then, that projected capital flows toward the poor countries are *not* likely (under present arrangements) to permit them to enjoy an "import surplus" large enough to support their "target" growth rates. This finding has led to an intense search for ways and means of avoiding the projected "residual exchange gaps" just described. Suggested methods for coping with the problem tend to place the burden of adjustment on the advanced countries. This follows from the emphasis placed on the alleged irreducibility of the typical developing country's import coefficient and the rather one-sided stress placed on demand side limits to its export potential. The most frequently mentioned and presumably sorely needed international economic reforms may be lumped under three broad headings:

1) Trade reforms designed to improve the import purchasing power derived from a given volume of exports emanating from the developing countries. This would include the various well-known proposals to stabilize, at historically high levels, the prices paid for the principal primary product exports of the less developed areas. It also includes a host of suggested commercial policy reforms, with "one way free trade" providing the logical limit.[26]

2) Measures designed to multiply and widen the markets available to the developing countries. This would include such items as: a) limiting the excessive protection and/or subsidization given to competing primary product producers in the advanced countries (for example, U.S. sugar growers), b) opening the Communist Bloc economies to a greater volume of the developing nations' exports, c) destroying the maze of tariff and other commercial barriers facing would-be exporters of manufactured goods in the poor countries.

3) Measures to increase the volume of long-term international capital flowing toward the poor countries, and to lighten the service burden connected with it.

The foregoing listing of suggested reforms is by no means exhaustive. A comprehensive, yet concise, treatment of the subject is contained in a U.N. publication.[27]

The underdeveloped countries undoubtedly stand to gain by pressing for such global trade reforms and for a greater volume of less expensive aid, for more extensive grants, and so on. Here and there some relatively minor concessions have already been made, with the recent coffee agreement providing a case in point. By and large, however, especially with reference to the prospects for a substantial increase in the volume of official capital likely to flow toward the poor nations in the near future, the outlook is anything but promising. In the United States, for example, foreign aid ranks last in polls of the citizenry concerning the popularity of various major government spending programs.[28] There has been a sharp drop in the share of the U.S. gross national product devoted to foreign aid since 1961.[29] The same is true of the recent behavior of the group of rich nations that makes up the Development Assistance Committee (DAC) of the Organization for Economic Cooperation and Development (OECD).[30] Thus, the total net flow of long-term capital from the rich non-Communist countries toward the poor nations declined in absolute volume between 1961 and 1964, contrary to Balassa's (perhaps overly optimistic) assumption that it would increase as the national incomes of the rich nations rose during the 1960's.[31] The most that can be said, therefore, is that the rich countries may or may not eventually accede to demands for more extensive aid and trade concessions. Only time will tell.

Meanwhile, developing countries seriously interested in forcing the pace of their growth must do so in the world as it is and is likely to be in the immediate future. For individual countries, more degrees of freedom exist than the foregoing group-focused models imply. A few developing countries, deeply involved in international trade, have already proved that ambitious growth targets are attainable under existing arrangements in world commerce. Mexico's recent experience in this respect is interpreted in the following chapters.

Notes to Chapter 1

1. Gerald M. Meier, International Trade and Development (New York: Harper & Row, 1963), p. 74.

2. Bela Balassa, Trade Prospects for Developing Countries (Homewood, Ill.: Richard D. Irwin, Inc., 1964).

3. See Chapter 2.

4. Balassa, op. cit., pp. 71-72, reviews the target growth rates employed in the most recent national development plans of nineteen poor countries.

5. See, for example, Item Number 1 in Title I of, "The Charter of Punta del Este, Establishing an Alliance for Progress," as reproduced in Lincoln Gordon, A New Deal for Latin America (Cambridge: Harvard University Press, 1963), pp. 119-20.

6. A theme, for example, of Barbara Ward's, The Rich Nations and the Poor Nations (New York: W.W. Norton & Co., 1962).

7. This norm is cited and employed in all recent United Nations "trade-gap" studies. For example: United Nations (hereinafter, U.N.) Secretariat, "Trade Needs of Developing Countries for Their Accelerated Economic Growth," World Economic Survey, 1963, Part I (New York: United Nations, 1964), pp. 29-42. It is also taken as the normative goal in The Contracting Parties of the General Agreement on Tariffs and Trades' (hereinafter, GATT), "Foreign Trade and Long-Term Economic Growth of Developing Countries," International Trade, 1961 (Geneva: GATT, 1962), pp. 8-22.

8. Balassa, op. cit., pp. 123-27.

9. The phrase is taken from p. 18 of the GATT "trade-gap" study, op. cit.

10. Balassa, op. cit., pp. 67-80.

11. Ibid.

12. Report by the Secretary-General [Raul Prebisch] of the United Nations Conference on Trade and Development, Towards a New Trade Policy for Development (New York: United Nations, 1964), p. 4.

13. The various U.N. agencies subscribe to the debatable "secular deterioration hypothesis." For a brief critical review of it, see Meier, op. cit., pp. 55-63.

14. See U.N. Secretariat, op. cit., pp. 55-63.

15. Balassa, op. cit., pp. 43-65, 131-338.

16. U.N. Secretariat, op. cit., p. 34.

17. Balassa, op. cit., p. 104.

18. Proceedings of a Chatham House Conference, Bellagio, 16-24 September, 1963, New Directions for World Trade (London: Oxford University Press, 1964), p. 201. The high estimate ($20 billion) is taken directly from the U.N. study, while the lower estimate ($13 billion) is drawn on the assumption that more favorable conditions than those envisioned by the U.N. will develop.

19. Heavy net outflows of investment service payments are the largest deficit item on the service accounts.

20. Drawing down exchange reserves, another possible source of funds to close the gap, is not a feasible solution for the less-developed countries as a group. Their holdings of such reserves are simply too low to allow it.

21. Based on Balassa's estimate of a $12 billion gap vs. about $44 billion in "import needs," op. cit., pp. 94-95, 103, 123.

22. Based on the U.N. finding of a $20 billion gap vs. $51 billion in "import needs," U.N. Secretariat, op. cit., p. 31.

23. Balassa, op. cit., p. 123. See below for a discussion of Balassa's assumptions about future capital flows toward the poor countries.

24. U.N. Secretariat, op. cit., p. 31.

25. Ibid., p. 39. Also see Balassa's critique of the U.N. Secretariat's technique, Balassa, op. cit., pp. 96-97, 105.

26. An idea suggested by Alfred C. Neal, "New Economic Policies for the West," Foreign Affairs, January, 1961, p. 252.

27. Report by the Secretary-General of the United Nations Conference on Trade and Development.

28. Eva Mueller, "Public Attitudes Toward Fiscal Programs," Quarterly Journal of Economics, LXXVII, No. 2, May, 1963, p. 215.

29. For a detailed analysis and discussion of this point, see The New York Times, February 6, 1966, Section E, p. 3.

30. George D. Woods, "The Development Decade," Foreign Affairs, January, 1966, p. 214.

31. Specifically, the member countries of DAC (i.e., the United States, Canada, Japan, and the Scandinavian and West European nations) in 1961 transferred $8.73 billion (U.S.) toward the poor countries. The latest estimates available show that by 1964 the comparable figure was $8.65 billion. This includes net transfers on both public and private account. See OECD, Development Assistance Efforts and Policies, 1965 Review (Paris: OECD, September, 1965), p. 127, Table 3. Compare this finding to Balassa's capital flow assumptions, op. cit., p. 121.

CHAPTER 2 MEXICO'S ECONOMIC DEVELOPMENT SINCE 1940

RATES OF GROWTH OF THE GNP AND THE LEVEL AND COMPOSITION OF PUBLIC INVESTMENT

Over the past quarter of a century, Mexico has experienced a period of rapid and sustained economic growth. The latest revisions of the best official data available indicate that the real gross national product (GNP) has expanded at a compound average rate of about 6 per cent per year since 1940. (See Table 1.) In the face of a rising population growth rate, now approaching 3.5 per cent per year, this has yielded increments in output of approximately 3 per cent per capita. In terms of these broad measures of economic progress, Mexico has clearly demonstrated its ability to meet the basic growth targets commonly cited at international forums. No prolonged or pronounced recessions in the level of economic activity occurred during the period in question.[1]

Data describing the types of expenditure on the GNP are unfortunately very poor, and a series estimating the factoral distribution of the national income is not kept at all. Aggregate public and private gross fixed investment spending are estimated, however.[2] The investment coefficient deviated little from its average level of about one-tenth of GNP during World War II.[3] By the end of the 1940's, it had risen to an average level of about one-seventh of GNP.[4] Since then, there has been no distinct rise or fall in the average share of the product devoted to investment, and year-to-year fluctuations have generally been rather mild. The relatively stable performance of the over-all investment coefficient may be attributable in large measure to the countercyclical nature of public investment spending vis-à-vis private investment outlays.[5] Public investment outlays have accounted for as little as one-third of total investment and for as much as two-thirds of it since 1940. Because of the importance usually attributed to public investment programs in discussions of the development of poor countries, Mexico's recent efforts along these lines will be briefly analyzed.

Table 1

Rates of Growth of the Gross National Product of Mexico, 1940-65
(In real terms at 1950 prices)

Period	Compound Average Annual Growth Rate of	
	GNP	GNP Per Capita
1940-44	7.6	5.1
1945-49	4.9	2.1
1940-49	6.3	3.6
1950-54	6.0	3.1
1955-59	6.3	3.1
1950-59	6.2	3.1
1960	7.9	4.6
1961	3.5	.1
1962	4.8	1.5
1963	6.3	2.9
1964	10.0	6.6
1965	5.4	2.1
1960-65	6.3	3.0
1940-65	6.2	3.4

Source: Table 39.

Table 2 summarizes public sector investments, by object of expenditure, since 1935. A few types of expenditures have clearly received the lion's share of scarce investment resources. Irrigation works have been a perennial favorite in this connection. About eight million acres of land have been opened or improved as a result of such outlays. (See Table 3.) Roughly, three-fourths of this land is located in a handful of far northern states.[6] About two-fifths of total production in the agricultural sector (in 1960) was attributable to crops grown on publicly watered land.[7] Moreover, about three-fifths of the crops grown on such land has been exported in recent years.

Table 2

Investments of the Public Sector in Mexico, 1935-63

	1935-40	1941-46	1947-52	1953-58	1959-63
Total Outlays (million pesos)	947	4309	14091	29674	50729
			Percentage Distribution		
Agricultural Investments	17.8	15.7	22.0	13.0	8.9
Irrigation works	16.8	15.0	16.2	12.2	8.5
Other	1.0	.7	5.8	.8	.4
Industrial Investments	9.3	10.2	18.9	30.3	35.3
Electricity	.7	2.2	6.8	6.7	17.3
Gas and oil	8.6	8.0	12.0	19.8	13.7
Other	---	---	.1	3.7	4.3
Communication and Transportation Investments	51.4	51.6	40.2	36.3	30.2
Roads	18.9	23.3	16.0	14.7	11.9
Railroads	29.4	26.0	21.3	16.0	11.4
Other	3.1	2.3	2.9	5.7	6.8
Social Investments	8.3	12.9	13.3	14.3	21.3
Public housing	---	---	1.5	1.5	4.9
Hospitals	.7	1.5	1.5	1.5	4.8
School and research facilities	2.4	1.2	3.0	2.5	2.5
Other	5.2	10.2	7.3	8.7	9.1

Table 2 (Continued)

	1935-40	1941-46	1947-52	1953-58	1959-63
Miscellaneous	13.3	9.5	5.6	6.1	4.2

Notes: 1935-61 data include investment outlays of state and local governments plus the investments of decentralized agencies and state-owned enterprises. The data for 1962 and 1963 omit outlays of state and local governments; the latter are relatively unimportant. Figures may not add due to rounding. --- indicates insignificant quantities.

Sources: Aniceto Rosas and Roberto Santillán, Teoría General de las Finanzas Públicas y el Caso de México (México: Universidad Nacional Autonoma de México, 1962), p. 219. 1962-63: Banco Nacional de Comercio Exterior, Comercio Exterior, Vol. XV, No. 2, February, 1965, p. 118.

The heavy investments in road building produced the phenomenal expansion in the highway network shown in Table 3. The railroad investments, however, were not used to expand the government-owned rail grid, but rather to reshape and modernize it to permit the almost threefold rise in the volume of freight carried in recent years, compared with the 1940 level, also shown in Table 3.

With Mexico's hostile climate and topography, few outside observers have questioned the general magnitude of the government's effort to improve the transportation grid and make up for a grossly inadequate endowment of arable land.[8] Criticism has often been brought to bear, however, on various aspects of the execution of such programs.

The Mexican government now also holds a virtual monopoly on the basic sources of power for industrial and residential uses.[9] Investments in the petroleum industry and in the recently nationalized electric power industry are shown in Table 2 and the production trends in these industries are shown in Table 3.

Until quite recently, the so-called social investments, shown in Table 2, received scant attention compared with the programs mentioned above. Beginning with the need for shelter, the Bank of Mexico estimates that one million additional units of public housing in urban areas alone would barely provide for the most urgent needs in that respect.[10] The 1960 census reports that roughly half the entire population lived in one-room dwellings at that time. Moreover, the census also reported that only one-fourth of all dwellings had piped in water and sewer connections, one-fifth had modern facilities for bathing, and one-sixth cooked with gas or electricity.[11] These data provide some indication of what remains to be done by way of providing basic public utility services to households. Finally, since the population in 1960 was almost twice as large as that of 1940, it is clear that the absolute magnitude of the effort required to satisfy these needs is growing. There are now <u>absolutely</u> more one-room dwellings without potable water, sewer connections, gas and electric service, and so on, than in 1940.

Considerable progress has been made in the fields of public health and education, however. Between 1940 and 1960, the general mortality rate declined from twenty-three to

Table 3

Results of Major Public Spending Programs, 1940-63

	1940	1950	1960	1963
Primary Education Programs				
Primary schools (thousands)	19	24	34	35
Primary school teachers (thousands)	40	66	117	119
Primary school students (thousands)	2,112	3,032	5,368	6,542
Irrigation Works (thousand hectares)				
Total area opened or improved	267	1,187	2,296	3,154[a]
New land only	147	676	1,408	1,722[a]
Power Development				
Installed electric generating capacity (thousand kw.)	681	1,235	3,021	4,192
Electric power produced (million kw-h.)	2,529	4,423	10,636	13,567
Petroleum industry output				
Crude oil (thousand bbls.)	44	74	109	122
Natural gas (million cubic meters)	1,049	1,762	9,664	11,371
Transport Development				
Billions of ton kilometers of rail freight moved	5.8	8.4	14.00	14.96
Rail network (kms.)	22,979	23,332	23,370	23,501
Road and highway (kms.)	9,929	21,422	45,089	56,237[a]
All-weather roads	8,286	19,557	37,691	50,462[a]
Gravel roads	1,643	1,865	7,398	5,775[a]

Notes: All figures are rounded. [a]Data refer to 1964 and are taken from the second source listed below.

Sources: Nacional Financiera, *50 años de Revolución Méxicana en cifras* (Mexico: Talleres Gráficos Nacionales, 1963), pp. 49, 74, 85, 174, 176, 178.

Nacional Financiera, *NAFIN en el Desarrollo Económico de México, 1934-64* (México: Nacional Financiera, 1965), pp. 20-23.

eleven persons per thousand,[12] while the functional literacy rate rose from 42 to 62 per cent of the population.[13] Nonetheless, most Mexicans cannot afford private personal medical care; and the Social Security Institute, which is the chief dispenser of "free" care for the poor, had only about one-tenth of the population under its aegis in 1960.

Table 3 also shows the progress in building primary schools, staffing them with teachers and enrolling school-age children. Much of the headway made to date in the struggle against illiteracy, and in meeting the skilled manpower needs of the nation, is traceable to the fact that Mexico has gradually raised the proportion of the Federal budget expenditures devoted to education. In recent years, about one-fifth of the budget has gone to the Ministry of Education while the military's share has fallen to one-tenth, in marked contrast to many other American republics.[14]

Focusing, for a moment, on the question of government taxation and expenditure, it should be noted that the various levels of government have yet to absorb as much as one-ninth of the GNP in taxes. This represents an unusually modest tax burden, even by the standards of poor countries.[15] Since most of the nation's gross private domestic investment is apparently financed out of reinvested earnings, it might be alleged that this low level of taxation has stimulated private investment spending and thereby promoted the development of new industries.[16] This, at any rate, is an explicit reason given for the generous tax exemptions extended under the various laws designed to promote the development of "new and necessary industries."[17]

In spite of the continuing low level of taxation, substantial progress has been made since the mid-1950's in finding less inflationary means of financing the ambitious public investment programs, as well as a rapidly rising level of recurrent budgetary expenditures. The problem has been complicated by the fact that the capital market in Mexico is still clearly underdeveloped, especially from the government's point of view, in that there is only a very limited free market for government bonds of any kind. Especially during the 1940's and early 1950's, the public sector financed a large part of its deficits via direct extensions of credit from the central bank to various public agencies, with predictable effects on the level of domestic prices.[18] Since the currency devaluation of

1954, however, a number of forces tending to reduce the inflationary bias in the economy have come into play.

First, there has been a substantial increase in the inflow of investment capital from abroad, on official account, leading to a rapid rise in the share of the public investment program that is externally financed.[19] Second, especially with regard to the debt issue of Nacional Financiera (hereinafter NAFIN), some improvement has been witnessed lately in the willingness of domestic private investors to buy government bonds. Third, a more sophisticated (and less inflationary) central bank policy has gradually been formulated. Thus, because of its inability to conduct extensive open market operations, the Bank of Mexico has instituted a complex set of portfolio requirements for the nation's commercial banks to control both the volume and kind of credit extended by the banking system. These controls have gradually been extended to cover other types of financial institutions. Though surely imperfect as a policy tool, the new style of monetary policy clearly represents an improvement over the cruder methods of the 1940's.[20]

Finally, turning briefly to the income side of the Federal budget, Mexico has in recent years made considerable progress relative to other Latin American countries in reducing its reliance on indirect taxes, as shown in Table 4.

Table 4

Income Taxes as a Percentage of Total Central Government Taxes

	1960	1963
All Latin America	35.7	36.1
Mexico	37.6	46.5

Source: IADB, Social Progress Trust Fund, 1964 (Washington, D.C.: IADB, 1965), p. 100.

This of course represents a major shift away from the more traditional sort of regressive taxes with obvious welfare implications.[21]

CHANGES IN THE INDUSTRIAL DISTRIBUTION OF THE GROSS PRODUCT AND THE LABOR FORCE

In addition to expanding rapidly in the aggregate, the Mexican economy has begun to shed the industrial and occupational profile of an underdeveloped country. A number of basic structural changes in the industrial distribution of the gross product and the labor force usually occur as a country progresses toward a more advanced level of economic development.[22] Among the most significant changes typically noted in this connection are (1) a relatively slow rate of expansion of production in agriculture and related primary activities, leading to a decline in that sector's share of the gross product; (2) a decline in the share of the labor force devoted to such activities; (3) a rise in the share of the labor force devoted to manufacturing; and (4) a relatively rapid expansion of production in the manufacturing sectors, leading to a rise in the share of gross product originating there.[23] Each of these phenomena has been witnessed in Mexico during the recent period of rapid growth, as shown in Tables 5 and 6.

Table 6 indicates that agriculture has been the slowest growing of all the major sectors, at least since 1950. The share of the labor force committed to such pursuits has also fallen and now accounts for just over one-half of the economically active population. These trends, of course, should not be interpreted as a sign of stagnation in such activities. The physical volume of production in the agricultural sectors has roughly tripled since 1940.[24] Also, a recent study by the U.N. Food and Agriculture Organization (hereinafter FAO) indicates that Mexico's performance as an agricultural producer, between 1952 and 1964, was surpassed by only two of the dozens of underdeveloped countries surveyed.[25] Table 7 provides an indication of the implications of trends in agricultural output when gauged in terms of domestic production of staple foods per person.

Turning to the manufacturing industries, it has already been mentioned that these have been the fastest growing sectors of the economy. (See Table 6.) They absorbed a steadily increasing proportion of the labor force while generating a growing share of the gross product. In spite of the substantial increase in the weight of these sectors, they have not yet played a decisive direct role in contributing to the nation's

Table 5

Occupational Structure, 1940-63
(Millions of persons)

	1940		1950		1960		1963	
	No.	%	No.	%	No.	%	No.	%
A. Total population	19,654		25,791		35,537		38,946	
B. Economically active	6,055		8,272		11,531		12,642	
C. B/A		30.8		32.1		32.4		32.5
D. Sectoral distribution		100.0		100.1		100.0		100.0
Agriculture[a]	3,831	63.3	4,824	58.3	6,239	54.1	6,690	52.9
Mining[b]	107	1.8	97	1.2	143	1.2	162	1.3
Manufacturing[c]	836	13.8	1,222	14.8	2,039	17.7	2,356	18.6
Transport and communications	149	2.4	211	2.5	358	3.1	426	3.4
Commerce	518	8.5	684	8.3	1,092	9.5	1,243	9.8
Other (incl. gov't.)	614	10.2	1,234	14.9	1,633	14.2	1,669	13.2

Notes: [a]"Agriculture" includes animal husbandry, forestry, and fishing.
[b]"Mining" includes the petroleum industry.
[c]"Manufacturing" includes the construction and electric power industries.
Columns may not total due to rounding.

Sources: For 1940 and 1950: Nacional Financiera, 50 años de Revolución Mexicana en cifras (México: Talleres Gráficos Nacionales, 1963), p. 29. For 1960 and 1963: Nacional Financiera, Informe Anual, 1964 (México: Nacional Financiera, 1965).

Table 6

Gross Domestic Product by Sector of Economic Activity, 1940-63
(In millions of pesos at 1950 market prices)

	1940		1950		1960		1963	
	Value	%	Value	%	Value	%	Value	%
Agriculture[a]	4,915	22	9,242	22	14,018	19	15,498	18
Index	53		100		152		168	
Mining[b]	1,705	8	2,372	6	3,994	5	4,482	5
Index	72		100		168		188	
Manufacturing[c]	4,489	20	10,094	24	20,609	28	24,810	28
Index	44		100		204		245	
Transportation and communication	955	4	1,988	5	3,638	5	3,829	5
Index	48		100		183		193	
Commerce	7,106	32	10,750	26	19,167	26	22,077	26
Index	66		100		178		205	
Other (incl. gov't.)	3,006	14	6,614	16	12,891	18	15,185	18
Total	22,216	--	41,060	--	74,317	--	85,829	--
Index	54		100		181		209	

Notes: [a]"Agriculture" includes animal husbandry, forestry, and fishing.
[b]"Mining" includes the petroleum industry.
[c]"Manufacturing" includes the construction and electric power industries.

Sources: All figures are based on official Mexican data collected by ECLA, and reported in the following places: For 1940: Raymond Vernon, The Dilemma of Mexico's Development (Cambridge: Harvard University Press, 1963), pp. 196-197. For 1950, 1960, 1963: ECLA Statistical Bulletin for Latin America, Vol. II, No. 1 (New York: ECLA, 1965), pp. 87-88.

export earnings. Most of the important products on the export list still are primary products. However, the manufacturing industries have materially aided in the stabilization of the nation's balance of payments situation--from the side of imports. This matter will be treated below when the process of import substitution is discussed.

Table 7

Production of Staple Foods in Mexico, 1930-63
(Thousand metric tons)

Year	Corn	Wheat	Beans	Rice	Total	Population (millions)	Kgs. Per Head
1930	1,377	370	83	75	1,905	16.55	115.1
1940	1,640	464	97	108	2,309	19.65	117.5
1950	3,122	587	250	187	4,146	25.79	160.7
1960	5,386	1,190	528	328	7,432	34.92	212.8
1963	6,424	1,786	700	266	9,176	38.95	235.6

Source: Tables 39 and 41.

ECONOMIC GROWTH AND THE DISTRIBUTION OF INCOME AND PUBLIC SERVICES

The Distribution of Income Among Families and Regions

The most pressing social issue concerning Mexico's recent developmental experience is pinpointed in the arguments of those who question its immediate welfare implications for the masses. Discussions of the subject tend to proceed in terms of emotion-laden generalities, usually unencumbered by relevant and reliable evidence, and for the best of all possible reasons. Almost no reliable data concerning the national distribution of income were gathered and reported until the mid-1950's. It is not surprising, therefore, to find that the few serious attempts to discuss trends in the distribution of income have tended to produce contradictory results, even when they have drawn on essentially the same set of crude source materials.[26]

Table 8

Distribution of Monthly Incomes of Families, by Region, July, 1958

Region	Average Family Income (Pesos)	Percentage of Families in Each Income Bracket							Percentage below grand mean[a] (825 pesos)
		Under 300	301-500	501-750	751-1000	1001-2000	2001-3000	3000+	
Rich Regions									
Baja Calif., N.									
Urban	2,066	d	1.4	6.7	12.0	44.2	22.6	13.0	11.7
Rural	1,775	d	d	24.9	23.0	31.5	9.3	11.3	31.8
Sonora									
Urban	1,361	d	9.2	14.4	23.7	39.5	5.9	7.2	30.7
Rural	1,100	6.1	16.6	19.0	15.8	32.8	6.9	2.8	46.4
Chihuahua[b]	1,365	7.2	24.3	13.6	14.0	21.7	8.7	5.5	54.3
Distrito Federal	1,449	6.9	16.3	13.4	17.2	24.0	8.0	9.2	46.8
All Mexico	825	d	47.5	19.7	12.6	14.0	3.5	2.7	71.0
Poor Regions									
Aguascalientes									
Urban	558	32.3	34.6	13.9	7.9	9.4	1.9	e	83.1
Rural	343	58.2	22.9	12.9	4.3	1.1	.7	e	95.2
Hidalgo									
Urban	847	8.8	20.5	22.2	23.2	20.8	4.4	e	58.6
Rural	386	47.2	29.8	19.9	2.8	.4	e	e	97.6
Oaxaca									
Urban	682	27.7	30.2	20.6	6.8	9.3	3.2	2.1	80.4
Rural	475	40.9	22.7	19.4	10.1	6.8	e	e	86.1

Notes to Table 8

Notes: Monetary income from all sources before taxes is included; income in kind is not.

[a]Families within national mean income bracket apportioned by interpolation.

[b]Urban and rural data combined in source.

[c]This row slightly understates the skewness of the distribution of family incomes since, in the poor states, all families with incomes above 1,000 pesos (or 2,000) were lumped together in the highest bracket tabulated, whereas, in the rich states, all families with incomes below 300 (or 500) pesos were lumped together.

[d]Included in subsequent columns.

[e]Included in previous columns.

Source: Secretaría de Industria y Comercio, *Ingresos y Egresos de la Población de México* (México, D. F.: Secretaria de Industria y Comercio, 1960), pp. 23-404.

Over the last few years, however, the flow of information concerning the distribution of income has increased in volume and in quality, making it possible to construct a reasonably consistent cross-sectional picture of the size distribution of the national income as of 1958-60. The data for this purpose are derived from a series of official studies published during the early 1960's.

In July of 1958, the Secretariat of Industry and Commerce conducted an extensive nationwide sample survey of individual family incomes.[27] The essential findings of the study are presented in condensed form in Table 8. The first column provides a sampling of the range of mean family incomes in various parts of the nation. The national mean monthly family income was 825 pesos, or about $66.00[28] Baja California del Norte was the richest state in terms of mean family incomes, and Aguascalientes the poorest. The contrast between mean urban family incomes in the former and mean rural family incomes in the latter was on the order of 6:1. In short, Mexico clearly has a profound "North-South" problem. Applying a measure of dispersion of mean incomes among regions, suggested by Williamson, permits an international comparison of the severity of Mexico's "North-South" problem. Where Williamson found a mean dispersion measure of 23.8 for his sample of 28 countries, our calculation based on Mexico's 1958 income survey data yielded a result of 32.4--higher, for example, than that calculated for Italy.[29] The regional mean incomes reported in the 1958 study ought to be corrected for regional differences in the cost of living, but adequate price indexes for making the adjustments simply do not exist. It is generally acknowledged, however, that it costs more to live in the richer states, especially in urban areas. Money income differentials therefore tend to overstate real differences among regions, although this bias is partially offset, in welfare terms, by the generally wider availability of public services in major cities and in the richer regions. (See Table 13 below.) With these reservations in mind, it seems reasonable to allege that marked regional variations in average family incomes warrant recognition as a basic dimension of a profound inequality in the size distribution of the national income among families. These regional differences essentially reflect wide variations in average productivity per man among regions. This matter has already been studied, as exhaustively as the available data permit, by Paul Lamartine Yates.[30] Table 9 provides a succinct summary of his findings concerning the interregional gradients in mean productivity per capita (or per worker) in agriculture, in industry, and in general; that is, in terms of a GNP per capita. These regional income and productivity differentials also help to explain why the streams of internal migration clearly funnel the population increments--generated in the less-developed regions--toward the Federal District (with its rapidly expanding industrial complex) and the booming far northern states.[31]

Table 9

Measures of Productivity by Region
and Type of Activity
(In pesos of the year indicated)

Region	Value Added Per Capita in Industry (1955)	Output Per Worker in Agriculture (1960)	GNP Per Capita (1960)
Rich Regions			
Distrito Federal	3,420	18,850	9,950
Nuevo León	2,890	--	7,070
Chihuahua	1,200	7,800	4,180
Coahuila	1,162	8,050	5,090
Sonora	825	19,600	6,360
Baja Calif., N.	1,030	33,800	11,900
Baja Calif., S.	960	12,100	4,700
Tamaulipas	1,149	12,450	5,840
National Mean	960	4,800	3,800
Poor Regions			
Oaxaca	98	1,970	1,022
Hidalgo	201	2,520	1,255
Querétaro	261	2,380	1,630
Guerrero	114	--	1,400
Tlaxcala	--	1,940	1,360
Zacatecas	--	2,440	1,765

Note: -- indicates data not reported in source.

Source: Paul Lamartine Yates, El Desarrollo Regional de México (Mexico: Talleres Gráficos Victoria, 1962), pp. 41, 54, 62.

Variations in regional mean income levels are compounded by sharply skewed intraregional distributions of income among families. This is also illustrated in Table 8, which arrays families across income brackets within regions, and in the Lorenz distribution of income within the few particular areas shown in Table 10. Thus, a populous, rich state, such as Chihuahua, had half its families sharing only 17.4 per cent of the total family incomes of the state in 1958. Roughly, similar results were detected in all other states, including even such very poor, heavily populated states as Oaxaca. The last column of Table 8 shows the percentage of families receiving incomes below the national (825 pesos) mean in various regions. Taking account of regional differences in nonmonetary "income in kind" would probably alter these findings very little.[32]

The far less elaborate income data collected in the 1960 census[33] support the general conclusions drawn on the basis of the 1958 sample survey findings. The greatest limitation of the census data lies in the fact that these data provide information only on labor incomes, and not on a family basis at that. These data do, however, array family heads according to their labor income brackets, as shown in Table 11. Note, again, the wide differences in mean incomes among regions and the sharply skewed intraregional distribution of these incomes. Table 12 conveys the distinct impression that quite a few families in Mexico probably enjoy a relatively luxurious style of life, even without the benefit of substantial nonlabor incomes.

Finally, in 1960, the Secretariat of Industry and Commerce conducted another sample survey of family incomes, confined in coverage to the sixteen principal cities of Mexico, housing about 25 per cent of the population.[34] It detected the same sort of skewness in the distribution of family incomes on an intracity basis. Differences in mean family incomes among such cities, however, varied by a relatively modest factor of up to 2-1/2:1.[35]

It appears, then, that the size of distribution of family incomes for Mexico as a whole is highly skewed because of the combined effects of a widely dispersed set of regional mean incomes, overlaid with deeply bowed Lorenz distributions of incomes about such means, within each state or territory. And the very bottom of the national income array is obviously

Table 10
Distribution of Monthly Family Incomes,
Selected Regions, July, 1958

A. Chihuahua (1960 Population: 1,226,793)

Income Brackets (pesos)	Families (number)	Total Income (millions of pesos)	Cumulative Data % of Families	Cumulative Data % of Total Income
300 or less	14,814	3.5	7.2	1.3
301-400	28,146	10.6	21.0	5.0
401-500	21,727	10.2	31.6	8.7
501-750	38,022	24.5	50.1	17.4
751-1000	28,640	24.6	64.1	26.2
1001-2000	44,442	65.0	85.8	49.5
2001-3000	17,777	45.0	94.5	65.5
3001-4000	7,901	28.3	98.3	75.5
4001+	3,457	68.1	100.0	100.0
Total	204,926	279.9	Mean family income = 1,365 pesos	

B. Distrito Federal (1960 Population: 4,870,876)

Income Brackets (pesos)	Families (number)	Total Income (millions of pesos)	Cumulative Data % of Families	Cumulative Data % of Total Income
300 or less	64,318	14.9	6.9	1.1
301-400	65,487	24.8	13.9	2.9
401-500	86,537	40.3	23.2	5.9
501-750	171,905	109.4	41.7	14.0
751-1000	160,210	143.0	58.8	24.6
1001-2000	223,359	326.2	82.8	48.8
2001-3000	74,843	191.3	90.8	62.9
3001+	85,368	500.4	100.0	100.0
Total	932,027	1,350.3	Mean family income = 1,449 pesos	

C. Oaxaca (1960 Population: 1,727,266)

Income Brackets (pesos)	Families (number)	Total Income (millions of pesos)	Cumulative Data % of Families	Cumulative Data % of Total Income
200 or less	57,414	9.2	16.4	5.1
201-300	76,304	20.1	38.2	16.2
301-400	53,851	19.5	53.5	26.9
401-500	31,477	14.4	62.5	34.9
501-750	68,915	43.8	82.2	58.9
751-1000	33,006	29.1	91.6	75.0
1001+	29,424	45.5	100.0	100.0
Total	350,391	181.7	Mean family income = 519 pesos	

Note: Monetary income from all sources before taxes is included; income in kind is not.

Source: Secretaría de Industria y Comercio, *Ingresos y Egresos de la Población de México* (México, D.F.: Secretaría de Industria y Comercio, 1960).

Table 11

Distribution of Monthly Labor Incomes Among Family Heads, by Region, June, 1960

Region	Average Income (in pesos)	Percentage of Family Heads in Each Income Bracket						
		Under 200	200-499	500-999	1000-1499	1500-2499	2500-4999	5000+
Rich Regions								
Baja Calif., N.	1,151	9.7	17.5	28.8	16.8	14.0	8.5	4.8
Chihuahua	756	9.8	40.0	29.0	7.8	6.4	4.2	2.6
Sonora	789	7.1	35.4	32.5	9.7	7.9	4.7	2.6
Distrito Federal	956	5.3	26.8	34.8	11.4	9.6	7.4	4.7
All of Mexico	626	24.0	42.6	19.8	5.4	4.0	2.5	1.7
Poor Regions								
Aguascalientes	497	23.9	41.1	22.1	5.9	3.6	1.9	1.4
Oaxaca	358	48.4	36.0	9.5	2.3	1.8	1.0	1.0
Hidalgo	354	34.5	48.8	10.8	2.4	1.9	.9	.8

Note: [a]The average income figure applies to all labor income earners. Income earned in return for labor services of any kind, before taxes, is included; income in kind is not. Data includes only those who responded to income questions of census takers.

Source: Secretaría de Industria y Comercio, Ingresos por Trabajo de la Población Económicamente Activa y Jefes de Familia (VIII Censo de Poblacion, 1960) (México, D.F.: Secretaría de Industria y Comercio, 1964), pp. 1-40.

heavily laced with the rural poor in the populous, relatively underdeveloped states of the Pacific South and the Central Plateau.

Table 12

The Lorenz Distribution of Monthly Labor Incomes, June, 1960

Income Brackets (pesos)	Labor Income Earners (thousands)	Total Labor Income (millions of pesos)	Cumulative Data: % of Income Earners	Cumulative Data: % of Total Income
Less than 200	1,727	194.5	24.0	4.3
200-499	3,068	953.7	66.6	25.5
500-999	1,423	966.1	86.4	46.9
1000-1499	387	433.9	91.8	56.5
1500-2499	285	512.1	95.8	67.8
2500-4999	183	601.5	98.3	81.2
5000-7499	89	518.8	99.6	92.7
7500-9999	19	159.8	99.8	96.3
10,000+	13	168.8	100.0	100.0
Total	7,195	4,509.3	Mean monthly labor income = 626 pesos	

Note: Income earned in return for labor services of any kind, before taxes, is included; income in kind is not. Data includes only those who responded to income questions of census takers.

Source: Secretaría de Industria y Comercio, Ingresos por Trabajo de la Población Económicamente Activa y Jefes de Familia (VIII Censo de Población, 1960) (México, D.F.: Secretaría de Industria y Comercio, 1964), pp. 1-40.

The Regional Distribution of Public Services

A study of the regional availability of basic public services suggests that the high income regions also tend to enjoy greater access to the nation's schools, health facilities, and public utilities of various kinds. This is illustrated in Table 13 where Column 6, labeled "Social Security Coverage," may be regarded as an indicator of the regional availability of public health services, since the Social Security Institute runs virtually all public hospitals and health clinics. The other columns in Table 13 clearly point to profound interregional differences in the availability of the various (mainly publicly supplied) services shown. At one extreme, the one-sixth of the population living in the immediate environs of the capitol appear to have the best of everything. Aside from their relatively high mean incomes (shown above), 95 per cent of the school age children were receiving some sort of instruction in 1960, while three out of four homes had access to modern sanitary facilities, and 45 per cent had gas or electric service connections. Furthermore, the major public health clinics, the largest low-cost housing projects, and so on, are all centered in the Federal District. These phenomena, prevalent on a slightly more modest scale in other major cities, lend credence to the notion that the plight of the urban poor, though more conspicuous to outsiders than that of their country cousins, is probably less intense in real terms.

In addition to their relatively low money incomes, most of the residents of such a predominantly rural poor state as Oaxaca appear to live without the amenities discussed above. And, as might be expected on an intraregional basis, there is a strong positive correlation between family income, educational achievements of family members, size of dwelling, utilities servicing the dwelling, and so on.[36]

The Government and the Distribution Problem

Drawing the foregoing pieces of information together, then, permits a balanced assessment of the social results of Mexico's recent Wirtschaftswunder. Output in the aggregate has expanded at a remarkable rate by any reasonable standard of comparison. Even in the face of a veritable population explosion, triggered by a precipitous decline in the crude death rate and the incidence of common endemic diseases, average levels of per capita output have more than doubled since 1940.[37] It was unfortunately not possible to determine the nature of trends in the size distribution of the growing national income. It has clearly been shown, however, that as of 1958-60, there were truly profound differences in mean levels of living among regions--both in terms of money

Table 13
Indicators of the Regional Availability of Basic Public Services, 1960

Region	Functional Literacy Rate (1)	Teachers Per 1,000 Children Aged 6-14 (2)	Percentage of Dwellings Serviced with: Running Water (3)	Sewer Connections (4)	Gas or Electricity (5)	Social Security Coverage (percentage of population) (6)
Rich Regions						
Distrito Federal	83.4[a]	20.2[a]	75.5[a]	73.4[a]	45.0	27.5[a]
Baja Calif., N.	81.1	13.8	50.3	32.0	52.8[a]	7.4
Nuevo León	80.7	16.3	53.4	45.4	41.3	19.6
Sonora	76.2	17.6	37.5	29.9	27.5	6.5
Chihuahua	74.9	16.0	41.8	34.8	26.3	14.9
National Average	62.2	13.3	32.3	28.9	17.5	9.3
Poor Regions						
Hidalgo	44.1	11.6	16.5	14.4	3.8	.8
Zacatecas	63.4	9.3	10.6	9.0	4.3	1.0
Guerrero	37.2	10.4	9.5	13.9	3.9	1.5
Chiapas	39.3	7.8	15.0	10.9	3.5	3.8
Oaxaca	40.9	8.9	7.4	7.4	2.0	7.4

Notes: Literacy rate refers only to the population of school age or above.
[a]Marks the region with the highest score for the nation with respect to the characteristic in question.

Sources: Columns (1),(3),(4),(5): Dirección General de Estadística, Compendio Estadístico, 1962 (México, D.F.: Dirección General de Estadística, 1963), pp. 20, 21, 48-50. Column (2): Dirección General de Estadística, Anuario Estadístico, 1962 (México, D.F.: Dirección General de Estadística, 1963), Cuadros 6.6, 6.36. Column (5): Instituto Méxicano del Seguro Social, direct communication.

incomes and in terms of access to public educational facilities, health centers, potable water supplies, power grids, and so on. And everywhere within regions, family incomes were widely scattered about the regional mean levels, with the poorer half of families in a given area rarely receiving as much as one-fifth of the total income available.

Three things ought to be considered by anyone who feels tempted to take the Mexican Government to task for failing to prevent the foregoing distributional problems from developing. First, although the government has clearly played a key role in promoting an unusually rapid rate of growth, its failure to promote a more equitable distribution of the fruits of progress is in a sense "normal" for a country at Mexico's stage of development. Specifically, consider the first problem of the profound interregional disparities in average levels of money income per family. This was identified above as a basic dimension of the over-all skew in the national size distribution of family incomes. Though the Mexican "North-South" problem appears severe, compared with the entire sample of countries gauged by Williamson,[38] it does not appear extraordinary compared with his smaller sub-sample of countries with per capita incomes comparable to those of Mexico.[39] The same applies to the over-all size distribution of income. The Kuznets study, for example, shows that poor countries tend to exhibit a highly skewed size distribution of income relative to that typically found in the advanced nations.[40]

Second, it may well be that the Mexicans would have had to accept a much lower rate of growth as the price of a concentrated effort to directly alleviate the extreme poverty of subsistence farmers in the underdeveloped hinterland. Consider, for example, the following prescription that the government might have followed in its attempt to deal with the problem of poverty on the land. It is a classic statement of an idyllic view of the "proper" course of the Revolution, cherished even today by many foreign and domestic intellectuals who question the course of action pursued by the government since President Cárdenas left office in 1940:

> The conclusion is obvious. The proposed program of large-scale investment for capital equipment as a basis for the growth of an industrial society can be achieved only by assuming a burden of cost greater than the country can support. If the Mexican government wishes to meet the basic issue confronting it--that of

finding a means of livelihood for its rapidly increasing population--it will have to devise an alternative program, one more consonant with Mexican realities....

It will be infinitely better for Mexico, however, if it turns its eyes to Switzerland and Denmark rather than to the United States as a model and seeks to find a way out on a local, parochial basis in thousands of little communities....

It /Mexico/ really needs a philosophy of little things. The Mexican rural school was that in its beginning, and upon that beginning it ought to build. There ought to be great emphasis upon little dams, not merely for small-scale irrigation, but also as means for the development of small lakes.... Each of these ponds, in addition to all other ends it would serve, could easily become a project for fish-farming, now sufficiently well developed to be taken over by any community that has even the tiniest running brook. Mexico ought to take over and expand the program developed by the state of Missouri. It has been established that an acre pond will supply six hundred pounds of fish annually with a little care and a small expense.[41]

With the advantage of two decades of hindsight to draw on, it seems clear that Mexico has done fairly well by explicitly ignoring such advice. The large-scale capital investments have been made, industrialization has been pushed, large-scale irrigation projects have been emphasized, and the roads and the railroads basically connect the rich northern region to the industrial heartland around the capitol. The rural communities have not been destroyed, only ignored relative to the investments made in urban areas and highly developed areas in the far north. Putting "little schools, roads and dams" in the thousands of rural communities would have prevented the government from concentrating its effort on building up Mexico's basic economic infrastructure. The government clearly chose to put off the issue of coming to grips with poverty in the thousands of little communities in the hinterland. Those communities are still there, and the flow of people toward the cities and the north has been compensated for by a high birth rate, which has maintained the man/land pressure in the poorest regions.

The third observation regarding the government's developmental policies and the pressing distribution problems is that there is much more to distribute now than in 1940; the basic economic infrastructure is in place, the tax base of the economy is broader, and so on. Thus, although the various fiscal programs have surely promoted inequalities in the past, there are distinct indications that the government is aware of these distribution problems and the urgent need to do something about them. As shown in Table 2 above, "social investments" are receiving a steadily larger share of the public investment program. The government is expanding the coverage of the income tax and relying on it more heavily. The emphasis in the irrigation programs has definitely shifted to the south and to small-scale projects in densely settled and very poor regions.[42] The government also shows every sign of earnestly seeking to fulfill its commitment to provide universal free public education for all school age children by 1970.[43] This of course means intensifying the educational effort in the hinterland where literacy rates are lowest.

The one great unsolved problem that complicates all others and becomes more pressing year by year is the ominous population growth rate. The Mexicans have yet to formulate a viable plan for coping with it. The major cities are growing at rates in excess of 5 per cent per year. Even the profound political stability the country has enjoyed in recent decades may be endangered if the birth rate is not lowered in the near future.

Notes to Chapter 2

1. In fact, the official series for the real GNP indicates that there has not been a year-to-year decline in aggregate output since 1940.

2. As far as other types of expenditures on the GNP are concerned, estimates of the net value of goods and services exported are rather crude, especially for periods prior to the late 1950's. No attempt is made to gauge aggregate inventory changes. Finally, private consumption spending is defined simply as what is left of GNP after deducting the aforementioned types of expenditures. No direct measures of aggregate consumer spending or its major components are available. For a brief technical discussion of Mexican national income accounting methods and practices, see: U.N., National Accounting Practices in Sixty Countries (New York: United

Nations, 1964), pp. 145-148.

3. See Table 40.

4. Ibid.

5. Ibid.

6. The same states Yates found to have far higher than average output per man in agriculture. (See Table 9.)

7. See Tables 48 and 50 in the Statistical Appendix, where it is also shown that these crops included most of the cotton crop (the number one commodity export), as well as most of the wheat crop (a major import substitute), and about one-third of the sugar grown in Mexico in 1960.

8. Less than 10 per cent of Mexico's total land area is currently used for agricultural purposes. One Mexican authority estimates that not more than 15 per cent of Mexico's land is even necessary to achieve the latter level of land use. See Armando Gonzalez Santos, La Agricultura: estructura y utilizacion de los recurcos (Mexico: Fondo de Cultura, 1957), pp. 35-53.

9. The petroleum industry was nationalized in 1938, the last privately owned power company was bought out in 1960.

10. Inter-American Development Bank (hereinafter, IADB), Social Progress Trust Fund, 1964 (Washington, D.C.: IADB, 1965), p. 117.

11. See Table 13 below and the sources cited therein.

12. See note 37 below. This phenomenon, of course, is the direct cause of the present "population explosion." The birth rate was and is quite high; roughly 45 persons per thousand.

13. Nacional Financiera, 50 años de Revolución Mexicana en cifras (México: Talleres Gráficos Nacionales, 1963), p. 174. Refers to Mexicans of school age or above.

14. Ibid., p. 172.

15. Alison M. Martin and W. A. Lewis, "Patterns of Public Revenue and Expenditure," The Manchester School of Economics and Social Studies, Vol. XXIV, No. 3, September, 1966, p. 205.

16. For an analysis of the financing of private investment in Mexico, see International Bank for Reconstruction and Development (hereinafter, IBRD), A Review of the Capital Market in Mexico, Report No. EC-104 (Washington, D.C.: IBRD, 1962).

17. For a detailed discussion of this point, see Stanford G. Ross and John B. Christensen, Tax Incentives for Industry in Mexico, Harvard Law School International Program in Taxation (Cambridge: Harvard University Press, 1959).

18. From this point forward, this discussion of Mexico's recent monetary policies essentially follows the recent excellent work on the subject by David H. Shelton. See his monograph entitled, "The [Mexican] Banking System: Money and the Goal of Growth," in Raymond Vernon (ed.), Public Policy and Private Enterprise in Mexico (Cambridge: Harvard University Press, 1964), pp. 111-175. Changes in the level of prices (i.e., the GNP deflator) are shown in Table 39 in the Statistical Appendix and in Shelton, op. cit., p. 126. Shelton and the IBRD report, op. cit., also present relevant data concerning trends in the money supply, government spending, etc.

19. See Table 15 below.

20. This, at any rate, is a general conclusion of the Shelton study, op. cit., pp. 172-89.

21. In recent years, the federal government has accounted for upward of four-fifths of total tax collections by all levels of government. As of 1945, the income tax only provided about one-fifth of the total tax income of the federal government.

22. Simon Kuznets, "Industrial Distribution of the National Product and Labor Force," Supplement to Vol. IV, No. 2 of Economic Development and Cultural Change, July, 1957.

23. Ibid., pp. 10, 20.

24. See Chapter 4 for a discussion of the importance of agricultural developments in terms of their impact on the nation's export capabilities.

25. FAO, "Special Feature," Monthly Bulletin of Agricultural Economics and Statistics, Vol. XIV, April, 1965, pp. 17-21. The nations that surpassed Mexico were Israel and Guatemala among roughly four dozen countries, when the index of total agricultural production is used. Three other poor countries more than matched the Mexican performance on a per capita basis.

26. Note the optimistic findings concerning trends during the early 1950's in Howard Cline, Mexico, Revolution to Evolution, 1940-60 (London: Oxford University Press, 1962), pp. 116, 343-44; vis à vis the relatively pessimistic findings of Ifigenia M. de Navarrete, La distribución del ingresso y el desarrollo económico de México (Mexico: D. F.: Universidad Nacional Autonoma de México, 1960). Both of the above studies use data from the 1950 census and a very small-scale family income survey conducted in 1956.

27. Secretaría de Industria y Comercio, Ingresos y Egresos de la Población de México (México, D. F.: Secretaría de Industria y Comercio, 1960). Modern sampling and interviewing techniques were used in the survey. The sample size was large, about 19,000 of the nation's some 6 million families were interviewed to provide significant regional mean income data.

28. Hereinafter, when values are expressed in "dollars" (or $), U.S. dollars are referred to without exception.

29. Jeffrey G. Williamson, "Regional Inequality and the Process of National Development," Economic Development and Cultural Change, Vol. XIII, No. 4, Part II, July, 1965, pp. 12, 16. The measure referred to is his "Mw" where:

$$M_w = \frac{\left| y_i - \bar{y} \right| \frac{f_i}{n}}{\bar{y}} x100 = 32.4 \text{ for Mexico in 1958.}$$

and: f_i = population of the ith region

n = national population

y_i = "income per capita" in the ith region

$\bar{y}$ = national income per capita

With Mexico, as in the case of some of Williamson's countries, "income per family" was used instead of "income per capita."

30. Paul Lamartine Yates, El Desarrollo Regional de México (Mexico: Talleres Gráficos Victoria, 1962), pp. 41-59.

31. For a discussion of this point, see Laura Randall, "Labour Migration and Mexican Economic Development," Social and Economic Studies, Vol. XI, March, 1962, pp. 73-81.

32. The 1958 sample survey does provide some limited data on income in kind, though not in sufficient detail to permit a precise estimate of its impact on the over-all distribution of family incomes. In a few of the poorest and most populous states (e.g., Hidalgo, Guerrero, Chiapas, Oaxaca), a significant portion of rural families live mainly or wholly outside the market nexus. These families produce most of what they consume. The general impression imparted by the income in kind data of the study is that including a reasonable estimate of it would have the effect of moving a substantial number of the poorest families upward within the very low income brackets (i.e., less than 400 pesos per family per month). The impact of this on the skewness of the distribution of family incomes would be offset to an unknown extent if one also considered the imputed (nonmonetary) incomes of the rich (e.g., from owner-occupied luxury housing).

33. The income data from the 1960 census (a total head count) was recently published in a special study: Secretaría de Industria y Comercio, Ingresos por Trabajo de la Población Económicamente Activa y Jefes de Familia (VIII Censo de Población, 1960) (México, D.F.: Secretaría de Industria y Comercio, 1964.)

34. Secretaría de Industria y Comercio, Las 16 Ciudades Principales de la República Mexicana, Ingresos y Egresos, 1960 (Mexico, D.F.: Secretaría de Industria y

Comercio, 1962).

35. Between the richest city (Tijuana, Baja Calif.) and the poorest (Morelia, Michoacán).

36. This conclusion is based on unpublished findings of a study of 1960 census samples, conducted by the graduate demography seminar at the University of Texas, in the spring of 1965. Information concerning the census sample and findings of the papers just mentioned is available at that institution's Population Research Center, Professor Harley Browning, Director.

37. The following changes were reported for the crude death rate and the death rates due to specific major diseases for the period 1940-60:

	1940	1960
Crude Death Rate per 1,000:	23.6	11.6
Deaths per 100,000 due to:		
a. Tuberculosis	56	23
b. Influenza	378	179
c. Gastroenteritis	487	196
d. Dysentery	55	17

Source: Nacional Financiera, 50 años de Revolución Mexicana en cifras (México: Talleres Gráficos Nacionales, 1963), pp. 25-26, 164.

38. See note 29 above. Roughly half of Williamson's sample consists of countries usually regarded as relatively rich or advanced nations.

39. Williamson, op. cit., p. 12. In fact, a main thesis of the Williamson study is that a spatial polarization of a nation's economic progress is a normal concomitant of the early stages of growth.

40. Simon Kuznets, "The Distribution of Income by Size," Economic Development and Cultural Change, Vol. XI, No. 2, Part II, January, 1963, pp. 45-50.

41. Frank Tannenbaum, Mexico: The Struggle for Peace and Bread (New York: Columbia University Press, 1946), pp. 242-43. Tannenbaum's theme was warmly endorsed by many of Mexico's leading intellectuals. For an

earlier rendition of the same theme, see Eyler Simpson, The Ejido, Mexico's Way Out (Chapel Hill: University of North Carolina Press, 1937).

42. Cline, op. cit., pp. 68-77.

43. IADB, op. cit., p. 376.

CHAPTER 3 THE DEVELOPMENT OF MEXICO'S EXTERNAL ECONOMIC POSITION

The remainder of this study interprets Mexico's adaptation to its external economic environment over the past quarter of a century. An explicit attempt is made to determine how the nation has fared with regard to the various external impediments to rapid growth envisioned in the "trade-gap" models. The analysis begins with a brief review of secular and cyclical changes in Mexico's international financial accounts.

THE BALANCE OF PAYMENTS SINCE 1939

Trends

Section I of Table 14 summarizes trends in the current account of Mexico's balance of payments.[1] Receipts and payments on account of visible and invisible trade are listed separately. Official estimates of the net capital inflow are shown in Section II, and Section IV indicates changes in the international liquidity of the Bank of Mexico. Section III indicates errors and omissions.

Various trends in the Mexican balance of payments are particularly interesting in terms of the "trade-gap" line of reasoning. There has been a persistent "unfavorable" balance of trade (in merchandise), on the average, since 1940 (line I-B-1 less line I-A-1). A passive balance of trade, it will be recalled, makes up roughly 60 per cent of the projected "trade-gap" in the studies analyzed above.[2] The remaining portions of the "trade-gaps" are attributed to large anticipated deficits under the service headings in the composite balance of payments of the underdeveloped countries. In the case of Mexico, such deficits have not developed. Rather, receipts on the service accounts have, on the average, exceeded payments by a considerable margin (lines I-A-2+3+4 less I-B-2 +3+4). Nonetheless, this unusual "service surplus" has not been as large as the passive balance of trade in merchandise.

Table 14A

Principal Elements of Mexico's Balance of Payments, 1939-65a

(Average annual figures in millions of dollars)

	1939-50	1951-57	1958-62	1963b	1964b	1965b
I. Balance on Current Account	- 41	- 53	- 183	- 103	- 406	- 360
A. Receipts	407	1,156	1,401	1,703	1,837	1,994
1. Merchandise Exports, f.o.b.	305	709	817	982	1,069	1,158
2. Travel Accounts	74	393	522	656	704	782
(Border Trade)			(367)	(446)	(463)	(505)
(Tourism)			(155)	(210)	(241)	(278)
3. Personal Remittances	22	31	35	30	29	12
4. Other (services)	6	23	27	35	35	42
B. Payments	-448	-1,209	-1,584	-1,806	-2,243	-2354
1. Merchandise Imports, c.i.f.	-380	- 918	-1,120	-1,240	-1,493	-1,560
2. Travel Accounts	-9	- 166	- 251	- 304	- 377	- 413
(Border Trade)			(- 223)	(- 265)	(- 277)	(- 294)
(Tourism)			(- 28)	(- 39)	(- 100)	(- 119)
3. Net Interest and Direct Investment Service Payments	- 55	- 98	- 173	- 212	- 291	- 297
4. Other (services)	- 5	- 27	- 40	- 50	- 82	- 84
II. Capital Movements	25	141	185	272	577	150
A. Net Long-Term Credits	27	115	200	307	514	181
B. Net Short-Term Credits	- 2	26	- 15	- 34	63	- 30
III. Errors and Omissions	36	- 56	- 8	- 59	- 139	188
IV. Change in Official Reserves (Sum of I+II+III)c	+20	+ 32	- 6	+ 110	+ 32	- 21

Table 14 (Continued)

Notes: [a]For a discussion of the accuracy and reliability of these data, see Appendix A. Columns may not total due to rounding.

[b]Preliminary figures.

[c] (+) indicates an accumulation of reserves

Sources: All data originate in the Balance of Payments Division, Bank of Mexico, as reported in the following places:

1964-65: Banco de México, Informe Anual, 1965, p. 99.

1958-63: private communication reporting recently revised data.

1953-57: Banco Nacional de Comercio Exterior, Comercio Exterior de México, 1958, p. 53.

1951-52: Banco de México, Informe Anual, 1954, p. 131.

1939-50: Report of the Combined Mexican Working Party, The Economic Development of Mexico (Baltimore: Johns Hopkins Press, 1953), pp. 348-353.

Therefore, a "trade-gap" on the current account has materialized, on the average, during the period in question (line I of Table 14).

But Mexico's current account deficit has been comparatively modest when gauged in terms of the expectations expressed in "trade-gap" studies. Specifically, the U.N. alleges that only about three-fifths of the "import needs" of poor countries could be financed via their current account earnings, if they achieved their growth target, under existing arrangements in world commerce. Balassa's far less pessimistic estimates imply that as much as five-sevenths of the imports needed to support target growth achievement might be earned via exports.[3]

Table 1 demonstrated that, since 1940, Mexico has more than matched the basic growth targets taken as norms in "trade-gap" studies. It would seem, therefore, that line II-B in Table 14 may reasonably be regarded as a de facto (maximum, ex post) estimate of the "irreducible import needs" consistent with target growth achievement in Mexico.[4]

If this ex post approximation of Mexico's "irreducible import needs" is compared with the size of the "trade-gap" experienced on current account (compare line I-B with line I in Table 14), it appears that Mexico has typically managed to earn upward of seven-eighths of the exchange needed to finance its "import needs," although the proportion of imports earned has fallen somewhat in recent years.[5]

Aside from their demonstrated ability to earn much of the exchange needed to finance a volume of imports consistent with the achievement of rapid growth, the Mexicans have lately experienced relatively little difficulty in attracting private and official foreign capital as a means of supplementing their exchange earnings. The net inflow of foreign capital is shown in Section II of Table 14. In fact, Mexico's success in drawing financial resources from abroad has led the largest of the foreign public lending agencies, the U.S. Agency for International Development (AID), to curtail its line of credit:

> U.S. support to other countries in Latin America varies according to each country's particular need and its own self-help activities.

> Both Mexico and Venezuela, with high rates of economic growth and ambitious development programs, have mobilized their own resources well and can now attract a substantial portion of their requirements for external assistance from sources other than AID.[6]

Chief among the "other sources" are the major multilateral international lending agencies.[7] Since almost all official loans have been on "hard" terms, and since the net inflow of them has lately mounted, the backflow of interest payments has become a major debit among the service items on current account.[8]

In recent years, the Mexican government's credit rating has become so well established that the treasury has been able to place substantial quantities of its own bonds in the New York market. Specifically, between July, 1963, and December, 1964, $100 million in Mexican Government bonds were sold in New York at a premium with a nominal interest rate of 6 per cent.[9]

Direct private foreign investment has also contributed to the growing <u>net</u> inflow of funds on the capital account.[10] The vast majority of it comes from the United States and, over the past three to four decades, a distinct shift has been witnessed in its industrial composition. Specifically, as of the late 1950's, U.S. corporations accounted for more than three-fourths of the book value of direct foreign investment in the Mexican economy,[11] and, between 1929 and 1959, the portion of such U.S. investments in manufacturing industries rose from under 2 per cent to roughly half the total.[12]

As in the case of interest payments connected with public borrowing, the backflow of service payments on private foreign investment has been mounting very rapidly. In fact, the Mexican Government estimates that the backflow of such payments has lately typically exceeded the inflow of new private investment on capital account.[13]

Because the term structure of the outstanding official debt is quite foreshortened, heavy amortization payments have been necessary in recent years.[14] Adding current service payments (the interest and direct investment service payments) to the amortization--and comparing the resulting total with earnings on the current account--indicates that Mexico has developed a very high "debt-service ratio" in recent years.[15] In light of the remarkably stable upward trend in export earnings,[16] Mexico's favorable credit rating in international financial circles, and the government's proved willingness and ability to keep a tight rein on the import situation, the service burden is not nearly as ominous as it would appear in a country less favorably situated. Nonetheless, Mexico does appear to face the rather unusual problem of having to consider limiting its borrowing abroad, of its own volition.

A final point with reference to the capital inflow is its expanding role as a source of funds in the public investment programs. Table 15 indicates the dimensions of the trend.

Table 15 B

Financing of Public Investment Programs, 1940-61
(Millions of pesos)

Year	Total	Internal Sources Value	Internal Sources Per Cent	External Sources Value	External Sources Per Cent
1940	336	336	100.0	---	---
1945	953	910	95.5	43	4.5
1950	2,666	2,329	87.4	337	12.6
1955	4,660	4,138	88.1	522	11.2
1961	10,460	6,753	64.6	3,707	35.4

Note: --- indicates an insignificant quantity.

Source: Aniceto Rosas and Roberto Santillan, Teoría General de las Finanzas Públicas y el Caso de México (México: Universidad Nacional Autonoma de México, 1962), p. 218.

Stability of the Payments Situation

The foregoing discussion attempted to isolate the basic features of Mexico's payments situation over the recent period of rapid growth--ignoring year-to-year developments of an essentially cyclical nature. Although no attempt will be made here to trace the development of Mexico's balance of payments on a year-by-year basis, a few notes on the subject are nevertheless in order. The World Bank Mission has already treated the period 1939-50 in some detail.[17] They found that Mexico's imports were severely curtailed between 1939 and 1943, owing to war-induced scarcities, whereas exports toward neighboring countries expanded rapidly, leading to a substantial accumulation of reserves.[18] This gave rise to what another investigator has aptly dubbed a large "deferred demand for imports."[19] After World War II, imports increased at an unusually rapid pace, exchange reserves were drawn down in a context of domestic price inflation, and the peso was devalued in 1949.[20] During the Korean War, imports were not restricted by the suppliers, as in World War II, and the ratio of imports to GNP (hereafter called the "import coefficient") reached its high point for the entire period since 1940.[21] Although the Bank of Mexico's reserves did not reach a critically low level, the peso was again devalued (to its present value of eight U.S. cents), in 1954. Since 1954, the external payments situation has been remarkably stable in comparison to the difficulties experienced in many other developing countries.[22] Marked declines in the import coefficient and the rate of domestic price inflation have served to ease the pressures on the payments situation from those quarters.[23] The Bank of Mexico has gradually improved its international liquidity. From 1960-64, only Venezuela, among the Latin American countries, held larger reserves than Mexico.[24]

THE TERMS OF TRADE

In terms of the "trade-gap" line of reasoning, deteriorating terms of trade reinforce the possibility that a developing country's growth aspirations may be frustrated owing to external economic difficulties. A given volume of exports generates a diminishing "earned capacity to import," in the face of such adverse movements in relative prices. This may cause the realized growth rate to fall short of that permitted by the domestic savings constraint, or other limiting factors, via allegedly inflexible relationships in production between domestic and imported inputs.[25] The following discussion brings together the readily available evidence on trends in Mexico's (registered, merchandise) commodity terms of trade for the 1940's, 1950's, and the early 1960's.

For the 1940's, the only useful terms of trade data

available are those calculated by the World Bank Mission, using U.S. data. Its coverage is limited to the registered merchandise trade between the United States and Mexico, which accounted, however, for more than 80 per cent of Mexico's imports and exports during that decade. (See Table 47.) Table 16 summarizes the World Bank Mission's findings.

Table 16 C

Mexico's Commodity Terms of Trade
with the United States, 1939-50
(1939 = 100)

Year	Unit Value of Exports	Unit Value of Imports	Terms of Trade
	(1)	(2)	(3) = (1)/(2)
1939-41 average	107.2	107.7	99.9
1945	161.5	163.9	98.5
1947	212.9	187.3	113.7
1950	271.7	178.9	151.5

Source: Report of the Combined Mexican Working Party, The Economic Development of Mexico (Baltimore: Johns Hopkins Press, 1953), p. 376.

For the period since 1950, the series in Table 17, compiled by the Economic Commission for Latin America (ECLA), on the basis of official customs data, is the best available.

Table 17 D

Mexico's Commodity Terms of Trade, 1950-63
(1958=100)

Year	Unit Value of Exports	Unit Value of Imports	Terms of Trade
	(1)	(2)	(3) = (1)/(2)
1950	100	76	132
1955	108	92	117
1958	100	100	100
1960	98	107	92
1963	106	101	105

Source: See Table 45.

Béla Balassa, Trade Prospects for Developing Countries, (Homewood, Ill.: Richard D. Irwin, Inc., 1964), p. 145.

Because of the lack of a consistent series of basic customs data covering the entire period in question,[26] a comparison of the ECLA and World Bank findings provides the only useful means of making a rough assessment of secular changes in Mexico's terms of trade. Table 18 links these two indexes and converts them to a 1950 base. It should be remembered that 1950 was an unusually favorable year for exporters of primary products.

Table 18 E

An Estimate of Trends in Mexico's Terms of Trade, 1939-63
(1950 = 100)

	1939-41	1945	1950	1955	1960	1963
Terms of Trade	66	65	100	89	70	80
Unit Value of Imports	46	92	100	121	141	133

Source: Tables 16 and 17.
C D

It appears that Mexico probably has not experienced a secular decline in its commodity terms of trade, at least during the period considered here. In fact, the country's terms of trade may even have improved a bit since 1940. This is in part because the average world prices for Mexico's most important commodity exports (gold excepted) have been substantially higher since World War II than they were between 1939 and 1941. (See Table 46.)

One other important factor has to be considered in attempting to determine whether Mexico has been engaging in trade in the face of adverse relative price movements. The so-called border trade and tourist trade have become a major source and use of foreign exchange in recent years. The terms at which the border and tourist trade are transacted ought to be considered in assessing trends in Mexico's overall terms of trade. The likely effect would be to force a pronounced upward revision in the terms of trade. This presumption is based on the fact that prices have generally risen far more rapidly on the Mexican side of the border than on the U.S. side. It reinforces the assertion that Mexico has probably not had to mount its recent growth effort in the face of a persistent or secular adverse trend in the terms of trade.

Finally, it has been alleged that "trade-gap" studies conjure up the image of a poor country attempting to grow rapidly while maintaining some semblance of external equilibrium, not only in the face of unfavorable relative price movements, but also under the pressure of an implacable rise in the "irreducible" import coefficient. Mexico has clearly not had to hurdle this double-barreled threat to its aspirations. Rather, it appears that the two factors have worked against each other. During the period between World War II and the Korean War, the terms of trade generally improved, while the import coefficient rose. Then, during the 1950's, the import coefficient declined as the terms of trade drifted downward.[27]

MEXICO'S IMPORTS

The remainder of this chapter presents a brief analysis of Mexico's "import needs" as they have developed since 1940. Aside from ordinary merchandise imports, Mexico also uses a substantial portion of its foreign exchange earnings to pay for unregistered imports of merchandise into the so-called border zones. Also, a relatively modest amount of exchange is spent abroad by Mexican tourists and in purchasing various sorts of commercial services from foreigners.[28]

The Border Trade and Tourism: Payments Aspects

In spite of its obvious importance to Mexico's external economic stability, the large and rapidly expanding border trade has been subjected to virtually no systematic study. Indeed, the Mexican Government itself knows relatively little about it and makes only rough estimates of its dimensions.[29] The excess of receipts over payments in these accounts is, of course, the reflection of Mexico's unusual "services surplus" in the balance of payments.

It is not very difficult to envision the basic factors that have created the environment for a rapid expansion of unrecorded imports into the border areas. The income data marshalled in Chapter 2 clearly indicate that families in the far northern regions enjoy incomes much above the national mean. The prosperity of the region is closely related to the geographical concentration of certain major export industries in the area plus, of course, the booming tourist industry.[30] Moreover, much to the chagrin of U.S. labor unions, many thousands of Mexicans cross the border daily to work in U.S. cities.[31] Although they work for low wages by U.S. standards, their income enables them to live well by Mexican standards. This, in turn, has contributed to the profound skewness in the interregional distribution of mean family incomes in Mexico noted in Chapter 2.

Because it is a relatively high-income region, the border area has long been a major net recipient of internal migrants, and the border citizens have been growing roughly three times as fast as the population at large, as shown in Table 19.

Table 19

Population Growth in Mexican Border Cities, 1950-60

City	1960 Population	Per Cent Change 1950 to 1960
Tijuana (Baja Calif., N.)	152,374	154
Mexicali (Baja Calif., N.)	174,540	170
Ensenada (Baja Calif., N.)	42,561	135
Nogales (Sonora)	44,992	63
Ciudad Juarez (Chihuahua)	262,119	114
Piedras Negras (Coahuila)	37,657	54
Nuevo Laredo (Tamaulipas)	92,627	61
Reynosa (Tamaulipas)	75,140	118
Matamoros (Tamaulipas)	92,327	102
All Mexico		33

Source: Banco Nacional de México, *Review of the Economic Situation of Mexico*, August, 1965, pp. 14, 15.

Evidently, then, relatively high per capita incomes and rapid population growth, augmented by immigration from other parts of the nation, have rapidly expanded the effective size of markets in the border region. Although it is true that Mexico produces a wide range of consumer goods, the major manufacturing industries are heavily concentrated in the

Federal District and, to a lesser extent, in Monterrey.[32] Both of these industrial complexes are economically far more distant from most of the major border cities than the highly developed adjacent U.S. production and distribution centers. Therefore, Mexican manufacturers are not in a position to compete effectively in one of their country's fastest growing markets.

The Mexican Government has long maintained special customs arrangements along the border, being most permissive in the far northwest where almost anything can enter the country duty free, unrecorded by Mexican customs officials.[33] Even at the eastern end of the border, where Monterrey is supposedly equipped to service border cities, a 200-peso ($16) blanket customs exemption applies.

It is not too difficult to discern the nature and causes of the growing volume of unrecorded border imports. Aside from imports of producers' goods to service the area's nascent industries, a growing number of relatively well-to-do border domiciled Mexicans are simply doing much of their consumption spending in adjacent U.S. cities, where large numbers of them also work.[34]

In a very real sense, there is substantial scope for promoting "import substitution" in the border areas. The Mexican Government has become acutely conscious of the potential import savings involved in bringing the booming border cities within the economic reach of domestic producers. It has improved communications between the North and the Central Plateau. It has begun to subsidize rail freight moving north out of the Federal District. A special program (La Programa Nacional Fronteriza) has been launched to clean up and service border cities more effectively.

Because of the sheer logistics problems involved in enforcement, the government would probably not enjoy much success in attempting to capture border markets simply by moving the normal customs frontier up to the border. To check the outflow of exchange on this count, it will have to encourage a northward shift in the center of gravity of the nation's production and distribution network, permitting Mexican goods to become readily available and competitive with U.S. products. This would involve reversing its past policies of aiding and abetting the centralization of industry in the capitol.[35]

Finally, the tourism item in the travel accounts on the payments side is of relatively minor importance. There are comparatively few Mexicans who have both the means and the desire to travel abroad. On the other hand, many Mexicans do go to the United States to work, and they are net savers, probably sending back enough dollars to offset the outflow due to tourists and students.[36]

Registered Merchandise Imports

In the discussion of the Mexican balance of payments, it was noted that there has not been a distinct secular trend in the import coefficient. The size of the import bundle relative to GNP rose between World War II and the Korean War and has declined to prewar levels since then.[37] There have, however, been some modest changes in the geographic distribution of Mexico's imports (by source) since the immediate prewar period. Table 47 indicates that Mexico became very heavily dependent on the United States for its imports during World War II. But by the early 1960's, the U.S. share had been cut to its prewar level of about two-thirds. Europe has yet to regain its prewar share of the Mexican market, and Mexico's purchases from its Latin American neighbors have clearly risen sharply, though they are still small in absolute volume and in relation to Mexico's exports to the latter area.

What is perhaps most intriguing about Mexico's import bundle is the dramatic change in its commodity composition. The fact that the Mexicans have lately been able to check the growth of the import bundle without restricting their growth rate is largely attributable to a continuing and pervasive process of import substitution, backed by conscious protectionist policies of the government.[38] The process of import substitution is one of the most interesting aspects of Mexico's recent development, and it ought to be carefully studied in considerable detail. It has not received the attention it deserves because of the magnitude of the data problems confronting the would-be investigator. The classification of the import tariff has undergone three major revisions since 1940 and countless minor changes. The most formidable data problem, however, lies on the side of home production. Only the grossest sort of home production information is available even for relatively recent periods. Any comprehensive attempt to relate changes in the mix of domestically produced goods to changes in the import bundle, therefore, appears destined to overburden the available data. It will not be attempted here.

Nevertheless, it is possible to gauge certain fundamental changes in the import mix, thanks to ECLA's diligent efforts to unravel the Mexican customs data, at least in terms of a broad classification scheme. The essence of the ECLA findings is summarized in Table 20.

Most noteworthy is the dramatic decline in the share of consumer durable and nondurable goods. This decline, of course, reflects the rapid diversification of light industry in Mexico since 1940. By 1953, the process had gone far enough that Sears Roebuck de México could purchase 80 per cent (by sales volume) of its full line of merchandise from almost 1,300 Mexican suppliers.[39] However, especially with respect to durables, a part of the foregoing decline is in part illusory in the sense that import substitution has merely involved importing "intermediate products" in the form of components for assembly in Mexico.[40] The case of automobiles is classic in this respect, with only about one-fifth of the value of the finished product being added in Mexico, as of 1960.[41] A similar situation may also pertain with regard to agricultural machinery (see Table 20), though major tractor components are produced in Mexico. Imports of transport machinery and equipment have lately been held in check with the establishment of integrated works for the production and assembly of railroad engines and rolling stock.

Truly dramatic progress has been made in expanding home production of basic construction materials. Since 1940, cement production increased roughly sevenfold, while pig iron and steel ingot production expanded more than tenfold--essentially driving such items off the import list.[42]

The country has also become essentially self-sufficient in fuels, with the rapid expansion of petroleum and coal production (shown in Table 41).[43] The rise in per capita home production of staple foods (shown in Table 7) has also made Mexico self-sufficient in food.

The broad categories of commodities that have gained weight in the import bundle are raw materials, intermediate products, and industrial machinery and equipment. Because of the somewhat ambiguous broad headings in the ECLA classification scheme, Table 21 conveys a more precise picture of

Table 20

Composition of Mexico's Officially Registered Imports, by Groups of Products, 1940-63[a]
(Percentages based on value figures adjusted to 1955 prices)

	1940	1945	1950	1955	1960	1963
Total registered imports[b]	100.0	100.0	100.0	100.0	100.0	100.0
Consumer goods	23.9	21.7	15.8	15.4	12.1	12.9
Nondurable	13.8	11.4	8.3	7.0	6.6	7.2
Durable	10.1	10.3	7.5	8.4	5.5	5.7
Fuels	2.6	2.7	4.1	7.9	4.1	2.6
Raw materials and intermediate products	42.0	38.3	39.4	37.2	44.4	52.3
Metallic	12.0	9.8	10.5	10.4	11.4	14.8
Nonmetallic	30.0	28.5	28.9	26.8	33.0	37.5
Capital goods	30.6	36.8	40.0	39.3	39.1	32.1
Construction materials	6.3	5.7	7.8	5.9	4.4	3.6
Agricultural machinery and equipment	3.4	3.5	4.6	5.0	3.2	2.4
Industrial machinery and equipment	13.8	23.7	23.1	22.7	24.0	22.4
Transport machinery and equipment	7.1	3.9	4.5	5.7	7.5	3.7

Notes: [a]The classification scheme is specified in ECLA, Statistical Bulletin for Latin America, Vol. I, No. 2, p. 217.

[b]Details may not add to precisely 100 per cent due to rounding and omissions of a very small "unclassified" category.

Sources: 1950-63: ECLA, Statistical Bulletin for Latin America, various issues; 1940, 1945: Unpublished ECLA data cited in Rafael Izquierdo, "Protectionism in Mexico," Public Policy and Private Enterprise in Mexico, Raymond Vernon (ed.) (Cambridge: Harvard University Press, 1964), p. 246.

the most important individual items on the import list, as of 1965:

Table 21

Mexico's Principal Merchandise Imports, 1965
(Millions of dollars)

Autos and auto parts and components	155.0
Complete industrial machinery installations	129.8
Trucks and components	48.5
Metallic parts of industrial machinery	37.0
Tractors and parts	34.3
Rubber, raw and synthetic	24.4
Wool	22.9
Natural and synthetic resins	20.6
Agricultural fertilizers	12.2
Newspaper	14.0
Airplanes and parts	11.9
Iron and steel tubes and pipes	8.2
Iron and steel sheets	9.6
Structural iron and steel shapes	32.2
Gases in cylinders	16.8
Railroad equipment	30.1
All other merchandise imports	952.5

Source: Banco de México, Informe Anual, 1965, pp. 104, 105.

With the present structure of the registered merchandise import bundle so heavily weighted toward complex intermediate and capital goods, future reductions in the import coefficient will be harder to achieve. The government has attacked the problem by attempting to force a rationalization of the auto industry, for example, reducing the number of allowable models, encouraging the standardization of parts, and so on. Also a few relatively simple merchandise import replacement opportunities still do remain, although the potential dollar saving is small. There is no reason why Mexico could not, for example, become self-sufficient in wool, newspaper, and rubber.

It may well be, however, that the best unexploited opportunity for further "import substitution" lies outside the registered import bundle altogether, in that the so-called unrecorded imports into the border area may be worth considering as an import replacement opportunity. This matter is discussed in Chapter 5.

Finally, as in the case of the development of the border trade, the process of import substitution has undoubtedly aggravated the income distribution problem discussed in Chapter 2, at least to the extent that interregional differences in mean family income levels contribute to the profound skew in the national size distribution of family incomes. The Yates study has clearly shown that the vast majority of the recent industrial investments in Mexico have been geographically concentrated in the capitol and, to a lesser extent, in Monterrey and the rest of the far north.[44] Almost without exception, the products of such industries have been marketed under an umbrella of tariff and/or quota protection, capturing (mainly urban) markets once supplied from abroad.[45] Even where "import substitution" has occurred in agriculture, for example, via the elimination of wheat from the import list, the incomes generated in the process have generally accrued to producers in the already well-to-do parts of the country. Moreover, the regional incidence of the benefits of expansion in the export base of the economy has also served to aggravate the problem of income distribution in Mexico.

Notes to Chapter 3

1. See Appendix A for comments regarding the reliability of the official balance of payments data.

2. See Chapter 1.

3. Hereinafter, the word imports is taken to mean imports of goods and services, unless specified otherwise. The same applies to the use of the word exports.

4. De facto payments for imports are referred to as a maximum estimate of Mexico's "irreducible import needs" because the U.N. growth target was surpassed and because there is undoubtedly still some scope for import substitution.

5. Since the aforementioned export performance exceeds the expectations voiced in "trade-gap" studies, considerable attention will be devoted to analyzing it in Chapter 4.

6. AID, U.S. Foreign Aid in the Alliance for Progress (Washington, D.C.: AID, 1965), p. 33.

7. All foreign loans to public agencies must be channeled through the government's development bank, Nacional Financiera (or NAFIN). For a detailed analysis of the inflow of official capital, see NAFIN, Nacional Financiera en el Desarrollo Económico de México, 1934-64 (México, D.F.: NAFIN, 1965), pp. 50-58.

8. It accounts for roughly one-third of the service payments under heading I-B-3 in Table 14.

9. See IADB, Social Progress Trust Fund, 1964 (Washington, D.C.: IADB, 1965), p. 372. NAFIN has also been able to sell its bonds abroad and to private investors. Thus, in 1960, the Prudential Insurance Company of America bought $100 million in NAFIN bonds at 6-7/8 per cent interest, redeemable in 1975. See U.N., Foreign Private Investments in the Latin America Free-Trade Area (New York: United Nations, 1961), p. 9.

10. In recent years, direct private foreign investment has typically accounted for a bit less than half the net inflow of funds on capital account, shown in Section II of Table 14.

11. See Banco de México, Informe Anual, 1959, p. 89.

12. See U.S. Department of Commerce, U.S. Investments in the Latin American Economy (Washington, D.C.: U.S. Government Printing Office, 1957), p. 180, and U.S. Department of Commerce, U.S. Business Investments in Foreign Countries (Washington, D.C.: U.S. Government Printing Office, 1961), p. 89. Over the same period, the share of U.S. investment in mining and petroleum declined from roughly two-thirds to about one-fifth. Between 1940 and 1959, the total book value of all U.S. investments doubled, as shown in the two places just cited.

13. The Bank of Mexico estimates that, between 1958 and 1963, almost three-fourths of the net earnings of foreign

companies were remitted abroad. See pp. 83, 90 of the Bank's Informe Anual, 1963.

14. These payments averaged about $180 million per year during the period 1958-63.

15. In 1963, for example, the ratio of service payments to "export" earnings was roughly one-third.

16. See Table 43.

17. Report of the Combined Mexican Working Party, The Economic Development of Mexico (Baltimore: Johns Hopkins Press, 1953), pp. 111-147.

18. Between 1939 and 1944, the Central Bank's liquidity position improved from $28 to $344 million. See International Monetary Fund, International Financial Statistics, September, 1951, p. 74.

19. Rafael Izquierdo, "Protectionism in Mexico," in Raymond Vernon (ed.), Public Policy and Private Enterprise in Mexico (Cambridge: Harvard University Press, 1964), p. 264.

20. International Monetary Fund, op. cit., p. 74. Reserves fell to $78 million by 1948.

21. See Table 44.

22. The peso has not been devalued since 1954, no multiple exchange rates are employed and the peso is freely convertible.

23. See Tables 39 and 44.

24. See International Monetary Fund, International Financial Statistics, Supplement to 1965/66 Issues (New York: International Monetary Fund, 1966), p. v.

25. For a detailed discussion of this point, see, for example: H.B. Chenery and M. Bruno, "Development Alternatives in an Open Economy," Economic Journal, March, 1962, pp. 79-103; R. McKinnon, "Foreign Exchange Constraints in Economic Development and Efficient Aid Allocation,"

Economic Journal, June, 1964, pp. 388-409 (especially p. 391); A. Manne, "Key Sectors of the Mexican Economy," Studies in Process Analysis, Cowles Foundation Monograph No. 18, Yale University (New York: John Wiley & Sons, Inc., 1963), pp. 379-400. For a thoughtful critique of the analyses of the foregoing type, see Hla Myint, "The 'Widening Trade Gap' of the Underdeveloped Countries: A Critical Review," paper presented to the Agricultural Development Council Conference, Wesleyan University, Conn., November 19-21, 1965.

26. The major problem lies in the frequent revisions of the tariff classification scheme. (See Appendix A.)

27. Compare Tables 18 and 44.

28. The ambiguous "other" services heading among the import items in the balance of payments consists mainly of such payments to foreign shipping companies, insurance companies, etc. It will not be analyzed here.

29. See the comments regarding the reliability of these data in Appendix A.

30. Chapter 4 treats these matters in considerable detail.

31. See Texas A.F.L. - C.I.O., Antonio Aguilar et al., vs. U.S. Commissioner of Immigration and Naturalization, U.S. Supreme Court, October, 1963, where it is alleged that there are thirty to fifty thousand "international commuter workers" in El Paso alone from the single border city, Ciudad Juarez.

32. See Paul Lamartine Yates, El Desarrollo Regional de México (México: Talleres Gráficos Victoria, 1962), pp. 34-37.

33. A few specific items, e.g., new autos, are explicitly prohibited. However, items imported duty free are taxed if they move into the interior. The customs frontier, for practical purposes, begins about 50 miles beyond the border in most places.

34. This, at any rate, is the general conclusion reached by Izquierdo who also noted that an unknown amount of

merchandise crossing the border is destined to be smuggled into the interior, op. cit., p. 249.

35. On this, see Yates, op. cit., pp. 20-24.

36. The recent curtailment of the "Bracero" program in the United States may eventually dry up this source of funds.

37. See Table 47.

38. The latter subject has been thoroughly analyzed by Izquierdo, op. cit., pp. 261-76.

39. Richardson Wood and Virginia Keyser, Sears Roebuck de México, S.A. (Washington, D.C.: National Planning Association, 1953), p. 1.

40. See Table 21, below, and Banco Nacional de México, Review of the Economic Situation of Mexico, May, 1965, pp. 8, 9.

41. See Izquierdo, op. cit., p. 285.

42. See Table 41.

43. Some fuel is exported, essentially offsetting imports.

44. This is the theme of Chapter III of the Yates study.

45. See Izquierdo, op. cit., p. 250.

CHAPTER 4 THE EXPORT SECTOR OF THE MEXICAN ECONOMY, 1940-64

Previous chapters have shown that Mexico has evidently been able to service an inflow of imports sufficiently large to permit the realization of a sustained and rapid rate of economic growth in the past twenty-five years. These imports have been financed via an expansion of the nation's "earned capacity to import" and a mounting inflow of capital from abroad.

GROWTH AND STRUCTURAL CHANGES IN THE EXPORT BASE OF THE MEXICAN ECONOMY

In terms of its capacity to generate foreign exchange earnings, the export sector of the Mexican economy has expanded rapidly, on the average, since 1940. This is illustrated in Columns (2) and (4) of Table 22, which show trends in the dollar value of total current account credits. The lower rates of growth, shown in Column (1), are based on dollar data deflated by a crude index of the unit value of imports.[1] The same table shows the extent to which the rate of growth of export earnings has varied over a number of sub-periods since 1940, with the late 1950's providing the only recent example of a rather prolonged period of relative stagnation. Absolute year-to-year declines in total export earnings have been infrequent, occurring only twice during the 1940's[2] and on three occasions since 1950.[3] Moreover, cyclical variations about the upward trend in Mexico's export earnings have been remarkably modest in comparison to the postwar experiences of most other countries.[4]

Another basic feature of the export sector's development is the divergence in the rate of growth of merchandise export earnings relative to total export earnings under the various current account headings.[5] A comparison of Columns (1) and (2) or (3) and (4), in Table 22, clearly shows that the merchandise export bundle has generally grown less rapidly than total export earnings. This, in turn, reflects the very rapid growth of earnings generated by the tourist industry and the border trade.

Table 22

Compound Average Annual Rates of Growth in Mexico's Export Earnings, 1940-63 (Per Cent)

	Merchandise Export Earnings Only (1)	Total Export Earnings (2)	"Capacity to Import" Based on Merchandise Exports (3)	"Capacity to Import" Based on Total Export Earnings (4)
1940-63	8-1/2	10	5	6-1/2
1950-63	5	7	2-1/2	4-1/2
1955-60	0	1-1/2	-3	-1-1/2
1955-63	3	3-1/2	1-1/2	2-1/2
1960-63	7-1/2	7-1/2	10	9-1/2

Notes: The growth rates shown in Columns (1) and (2) refer to U.S. dollar values of Mexico's import earnings, converted at average annual rates of exchange for the peso. The raw data for Column (1) are simply the sum of Lines (1) and (2) in Table 43, and the raw data for Column (2) are taken from the bottom line of the same table. The growth rates shown in Columns (3) and (4) are based, respectively, on the same raw data underlying Columns (1) and (2), deflated by the crude index of import prices, presented in Table 18. Column (3) roughly estimates the growth of Mexico's real "earned capacity to import," based on merchandise export earnings, and Column (4) estimates the same phenomenon, based on total "export" earnings, including earnings from the "export" of services. All growth rates were calculated, using compound interest tables, and have been rounded to the nearest one-half per cent.

In addition to the rising weight of services in the total export bundle, there have been profound changes in the relative weights of the most important items in the merchandise export bundle. Unlike many other developing countries, Mexico has been able to diversify its export base since World War II,[6] thereby reducing the threat of recurrent payments crises triggered by abrupt year-to-year changes in the world market prices of one or two primary commodities.[7]

Figure 1 disaggregates the merchandise export bundle. For selected years since 1940, it shows the percentage of merchandise export earnings generated by the most important export industries. Scanning Figure 1 from left to right provides an impression of the fundamental structural changes in the export base of the economy that have taken place since 1940.[8] The first salient feature that warrants attention is the secular rise in the relative importance of agricultural products. It is strictly a postwar phenomenon, without precedent in Mexico's economic history. During most of the postwar period, cotton and coffee, for example, have typically generated at least one-fourth of merchandise export earnings, whereas, before World War II, they usually accounted for about 5 per cent of these earnings. Other agricultural and related products have also contributed significant amounts to the total change in the volume of foreign exchange earned in recent years.

The rising relative importance of agricultural exports has come about mainly at the expense of certain historically significant mineral exports, especially metals. The configuration of the export bundle, as of 1940, is essentially the traditional one in terms of Mexico's economic history for many prior decades.[9]

Finally, in spite of a prolonged period of rapid industrialization, manufactured goods have yet to achieve a position of prominence on the export list. The merchandise export bundle still consists, in the main, of primary products.

Subsequent sections of this chapter analyze each of these broad structural features of Mexico's export sector in considerable detail. The amount of attention devoted to each export industry varies roughly with its current relative importance as a generator of foreign exchange earnings.

THE MAJOR EXPORT INDUSTRIES

The Tourist Industry and the Border Trade

Among the various components of the export base of the

Figure 1

The Composition of Mexico's Merchandise Exports
(U.S. dollar values disaggregated on a percentage basis)

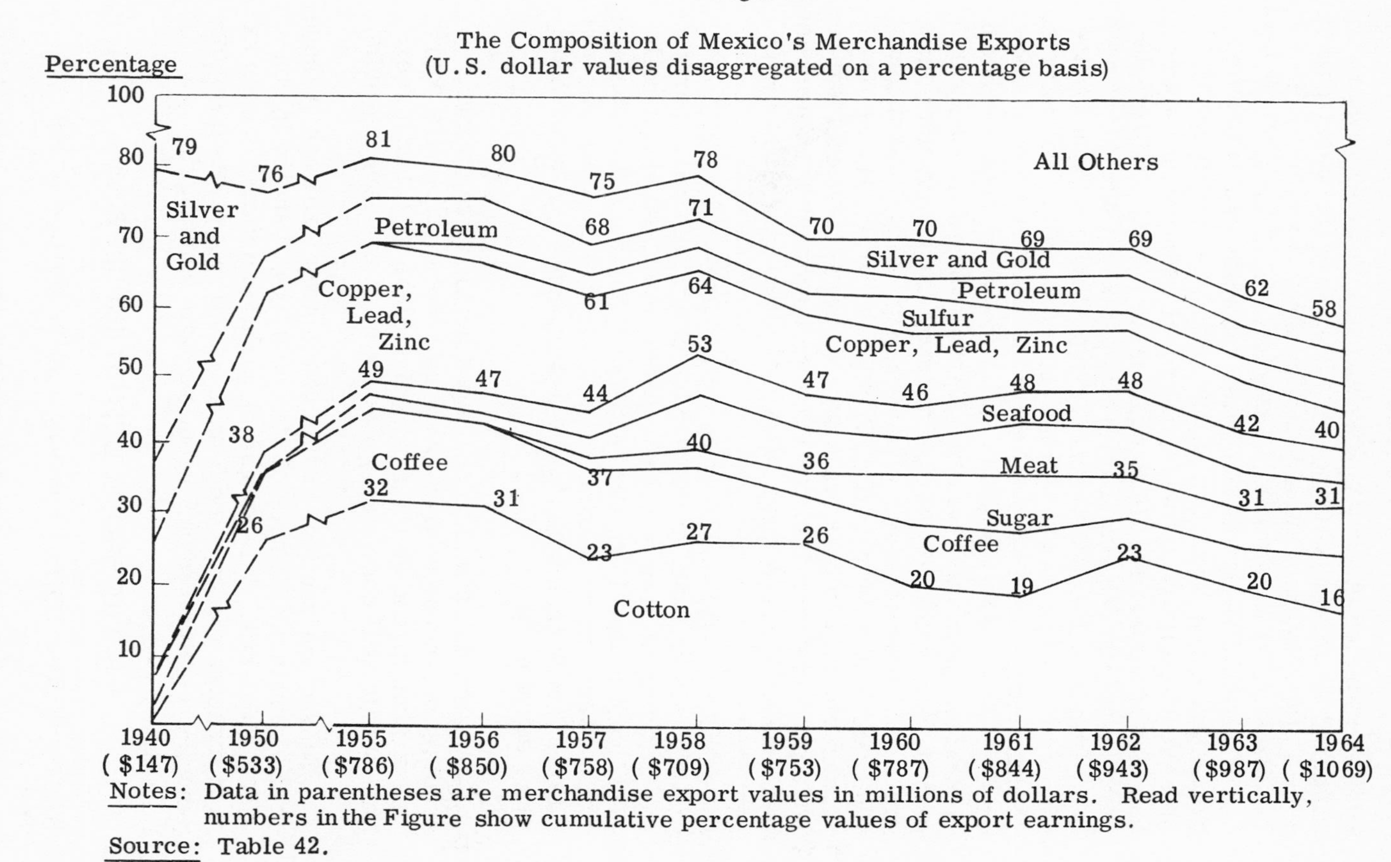

Notes: Data in parentheses are merchandise export values in millions of dollars. Read vertically, numbers in the Figure show cumulative percentage values of export earnings.

Source: Table 42.

Mexican economy, none rivals the tourist industry and the border trade as a source of foreign exchange earnings. Earnings in these travel accounts have grown more rapidly than any other credit item in the current account of the balance of payments. They have usually more than matched estimated exchange outflows under the current services headings, yielding a "trade-gap" on current account that is normally smaller than the "unfavorable" balance of (merchandise) trade.[10] Because they are essentially similar phenomena, the "tourism" and "border trade" aspects of earnings in the travel accounts will be examined together here, although much more is known about tourism than border trade.

Persons officially classified as tourists are those who visit Mexico for over seventy-two hours and/or enter the interior of the country. Such tourists must apply for a tourist card, providing useful bits of (ultimately published) information about themselves in the process. Their numbers have increased very rapidly, from roughly 100,000 per year at the close of World War II to over three-quarters of a million by the early 1960's.[11] About 95 per cent of them are Americans, who come in large part from states adjacent to Mexico, as is evident from Table 23.

Table 23

U.S. Tourists to Mexico, by State of Residence, 1961

Total Number of Tourists	803,405
From the U.S.	762,206
From Arizona	57,842
From California	170,967
From New Mexico	11,694
From Texas	228,202

Source: Secretaría de Industria y Comercio, Anuario Estadístico, 1960-61 (México: Secretaría de Industria y Comercio, 1963), pp. 106, 108.

Although no similar data are available covering the border visitors,[12] it seems reasonable to assume that they are even more likely to be Americans from nearby states.

Whereas all the border visitors by definition visit only the border zone, over half of the bona fide tourists report that Mexico City is their primary destination within Mexico.[13] Most of the remainder of the latter group give the rich northern states as their destination.[14]

During the early 1960's, just under half the tourists entered the country by auto, another two-fifths came by plane, and the remainder traveled via rail or ship. No information is available concerning the modes of travel used by border visitors. In the case of the various twin-cities, however (for example, Juarez-El Paso), it is quite common for people simply to walk across the border.

Turning to the rapidly rising total expenditures of the tourists and the border visitors, the available information concerning the former is again far superior, though the border visitors presumably spend about twice as much as the bona fide tourists. To estimate tourist expenditures, the Mexican Government simply multiplies its head count of tourists by a survey-determined estimate of average expenditure per tourist. Because neither a firm head count nor an up-to-date figure for expenditure per person is available with regard to the border visitors, a complex indirect method is used to derive the (frequently revised) estimates of their total expenditures, which are shown in the balance of payments.[15]

Since the overwhelming majority of foreign tourists and border visitors is American, it would be useful to examine certain aspects of the foreign travel market in the United States. At least since the early 1950's, American foreign travel expenditures have been rising roughly twice as rapidly as disposable personal income.[16] In other words, the income elasticity of demand for foreign travel services may be approximately two. The first row of data in Table 24 shows the total dollar results of this propensity to travel exhibited by American citizens. Clearly, the rapid rise of earnings in Mexico's travel accounts is in part attributable to the simple fact that the Mexican tourist industry has been offering its services in a truly dynamic market.

With peaceful conditions, a bit more than half of the American tourist dollar has been spent in Europe in recent decades, while the remainder has been spent in Canada and Mexico. During and immediately after World War II, Canada and Mexico together temporarily increased their share of the market at the expense of their European competitors for obvious reasons. By the end of the 1950's, however, Europe had more or less regained its traditional share of the market. However, there has been a secular rise in Mexico's share of the U.S. travel market. The Mexicans, it would seem, have somehow captured a growing share of the foreign travel dollar of the wealthy American tourist--mainly at the expense of Canada.[17]

Table 24

Foreign Travel Expenditures of U.S. Citizens, 1929-64[a]
(In millions of dollars)

	1929	1937	1947	1950	1955	1960	1964
Total ($)	483	348	573	754	1,153	1,733	2,216
Mexico ($)	36	44	140	172	255	365	480
% of Total	7	13	24	23	22	21	22
Canada ($)	178	156	241	261	306	380	550
% of Total	37	45	42	35	26	22	25
Overseas[b] ($)	269	148	192	321	592	988	1,186
% of Total	57	43	34	42	51	57	54

Notes: [a]The expenditures shown do not include payments to foreign-owned commercial carriers for transportation services.

[b]Expenditures "overseas" are heavily concentrated in Europe. Totals may not add to sums of parts due to rounding.

Sources: U.S. Bureau of the Census, Statistical Abstract of the United States: 1965 (Washington, D.C.: U.S. Government Printing Office, 1965), Table No. 293, p. 211; U.S. Department of Commerce, Survey of Current Business, Vol. XXXXV, No. 6, June, 1965, p. 26.

Two essentially complementary phenomena may be cited as explanatory variables of this experience. The first is that the economic center of gravity of the U.S. market has shifted toward Mexico. The same states that apparently provide most of the tourists and border visitors to Mexico have, since

1940, experienced higher than average gains in population and income, as is evident from Table 25.

Table 25

Changes in Population and Personal Income for Selected U.S. States, 1940-63 (Percentage changes for specified periods)

State	Population Growth 1940-50	Population Growth 1950-60	Changes in Total Personal Income 1940-63	Changes in Personal Income Per Capita 1940-63
Arizona	+50.1	+48.5	+1247	+430
California	+53.3	+73.7	+ 796	+354
New Mexico	+28.1	+39.6	+ 991	+511
Texas	+20.2	+24.2	+ 669	+479
United States	+14.5	+18.5	+ 488	+412

Source: U.S. Bureau of the Census, Statistical Abstract of the United States, 1965 (Washington, D.C.: U.S. Government Printing Office, 1965, Tables 8 and 459, pp. 13, 335.

For the tourist from Texas, California, and other parts of the rapidly growing southwestern region of the United States, Mexico is easily the least expensive foreign country to reach, in terms of transportation costs.[18] But an apparent enhanced locational advantage vis-à-vis the growing U.S. market at best provides a partial explanation of the dramatic expansion in Mexico's share of that market. Basic changes in Mexico's economic and political infrastructure constitute the other major item to be considered in this connection.

For the foreign tourists of the 1920's or even the 1930's, Mexico was a difficult place to reach and an unhealthy place to stay--featuring poor accommodations for such travelers. As of 1930, Mexico had less than 1,000 kilometers of first-rate all-weather roads. Since then, as a result of the heavy public investments in road construction,[19] Mexico has developed the most extensive highway network to be found anywhere in Latin America--56,237 kilometers in all, as of 1964.[20] A glance at any road map of Mexico reveals that the main trunk lines of the highway system are matched to incoming highways from the United States--providing a series of alternate routes from the northern border to the capitol--the major tourist oasis in the nation.[21] Having noted that almost half the foreign tourists travel by auto, it seems reasonable to assume that the extensive road-building program served to foster the growth of the tourist trade. It permitted Mexico to capitalize on its enhanced locational advantage, based on the mentioned changes in the U.S. travel market.

Certain other aspects of the public investment programs have had the same sort of effects as those just mentioned. For example, improvements in the water and sewerage systems of the major cities have reduced the threat of dysentery and other intestinal diseases which traditionally frighten tourists contemplating visits to poor countries.

Aside from the improvements in the economic infrastructure, the government has also made Mexico a place where foreigners may feel reasonably secure of life, limb, and property. In a part of the world well known for its political instability and recurrent civil disorders, Mexico has emerged as one of the few countries where the military stays in the barracks, while law and order is maintained in the streets and the countryside without resort to police state methods.

Were it not for government-sponsored improvements in the nation's relevant economic and political infrastructure, the impressive efforts of private entrepreneurs to expand the number of available and appropriate tourist hotels, eating places, and entertainment facilities surely would not have occurred.[22] In spite of their prodigious efforts to keep abreast of the rapidly growing influx of foreign visitors, however, much still remains to be done by way of providing adequate facilities for tourists, especially in the border cities.[23]

Two basic phenomena, then, may account for much of the remarkable growth of the Mexican tourist industry over the past three decades. The potential market available to the industry has expanded rapidly under the impact of rising population and incomes in the United States, especially in areas adjacent to Mexico. On the other hand, the Mexican Government has brought about certain indispensable changes in the country's economic and political infrastructure, which have had the effect of making Mexico a more accessible and a safer place for tourists to frequent. Coupled with a rapid increase in private investments in tourist accommodations, these factors help to explain how Mexico has managed to obtain a substantial share of the U.S. travel market since the 1930's.

Finally, with a few significant exceptions,[24] it is abundantly clear that the growing tourist industry has served to amplify the trends toward a regional concentration of wealth in the nation's capitol and the rich northern states. Paradoxically, many of the nation's magnificent archaeological sites are located in relatively impoverished parts of the country. The most famous Mayan ruins, for example, are located on the relatively underdeveloped Yucatán peninsula. The railroad and good all-weather roads reached that region only during the 1950's. As the hinterland in such places is made accessible via further public investment in roads and other facilities, the tourist industry may eventually serve to help raise living standards there, as has clearly been the case in the border regions.

Agricultural Products and Related Exports

Cotton

On the eve of World War II, Mexico was earning about $2 million per year, or less than 2 per cent of total exchange earnings, by way of its export effort in cotton.[25] Between 1958 and 1964, however, cotton exports provided exchange earnings on the order of $200 million per year, or roughly one-eighth of total receipts in the current account of the balance of payments.

In real terms, Mexico had to accomplish two things to bring about this increase in the volume of exchange earned via the sale of cotton abroad. First, a rapid increase in the size of the cotton export surplus had to be generated. Second, it had to be marketed in the face of what eventually became intensive competition from certain traditional cotton surplus nations, as well as a few other new suppliers among the world's cotton sellers.[26]

World War II isolated a number of the major cotton importing nations from their traditional sources of supply and thereby caused a marked contraction in the total volume of trade in the fiber, as can be seen in Table 26. Before the

Table 26

World Production, Consumption, and Exports of Cotton, 1929-64

(Annual average in thousands of bales)

	1925-29	1934-38	1945-49	1950-54	1955-59	1960-64
World Production	27,051	30,413	24,516	36,748	42,652	47,588
United States	14,933	12,389	11,131	14,521	12,760	14,743
India (and)	5,148	5,353	3,419	3,034	4,227	4,455
Pakistan				1,276	1,371	1,584
Egypt	1,535	1,846	1,292	1,752	1,714	2,002
Mexico	243	302	450	1,161	2,078	2,054
World Consumption	25,188[a]	29,609	26,917	35,419	42,522	46,763
United States	6,537[a]	6,454	9,181	9,325	8,672	8,657
India (and)	---	3,096	3,905	3,561	4,341	4,836
Pakistan	---			231	857	1,155
Egypt	---	73	221	297	428	582
Mexico	---	227	345	324	452	513
World Exports	14,332	12,743	8,764	12,476	13,737	16,669
United States	8,514	5,027	3,176	4,442	4,353	5,548
Per Cent	59	39	36	36	32	33
India (and)	2,938	2,746	923	174	314	233
Pakistan				997	549	451
Per Cent	20	22	11	9	6	4
Egypt	1,512	1,746	1,287	1,465	1,220	1,461
Per Cent	11	14	15	12	9	9
Mexico	93	105	234	863	1,556	1,539
Per Cent	1	1	3	7	11	9

Notes to Table 26

Notes: Export data are gross of imports. Cotton imports are negligible in the cases of the United States, Egypt, Pakistan, and Mexico. India's imports are substantial, however. Data refer to five-year periods terminating in July of the last cited years. All data are expressed in standard 478 pound bales except for the United States where cotton is counted in "running bales," typically weighing slightly less than 478 pounds.

---indicates data not reported in sources.

Sources: International Cotton Advisory Committee, Cotton World Statistics, Quarterly Bulletin, April, 1959, pp. 12-41; July, 1962, pp. 8-18; October, 1965, pp. 8-18.

[a]These data, not reported in the above sources, are comparable and have been taken from U.S. Department of Agriculture, Economic Research Service, Statistics on Cotton and Related Data, 1925-62 (Washington, D.C.: U.S. Government Printing Office, April, 1963), p. 37.

war, about twelve to fourteen million bales of cotton crossed national frontiers in a "normal" year.[27] Mexico's shipments usually amounted to less than 1 per cent of the total. As the volume of trade slowly regained its prewar dimensions during the late 1940's and early 1950's, Mexico partially replaced a number of the traditionally most important sellers in their major markets. By the mid-1950's, Mexican cotton exports accounted for about one-tenth of the volume of world trade. In the process, cotton became (and remains) the nation's principal commodity export.

Along with a number of other once minor suppliers (for example, Brazil, Peru, Syria, Sudan), Mexico was able to expand its share of the market in a context of historically high prices essentially because the United States, the largest of the major traditional suppliers, adopted domestic policies that reduced its exportable supply compared with earlier periods.[28]

The agricultural policies inaugurated during the 1930's, and pursued with vigor after World War II, were fundamentally designed to guarantee U.S. cotton farmers higher incomes in return for smaller crops. To this end, subsidized prices were paid to domestic growers in return for their compliance with the acreage restriction programs. Farmers responded to the combination of subsidized prices and acreage restrictions by rapidly improving yields per acre--as shown in Table 27. Nonetheless, total production has, on the average, been held to the levels experienced in prewar periods--in the face of a level of home consumption two to three million bales above prewar levels--yielding historically modest-sized U.S. export surpluses. In addition, especially before 1956 (when the export subsidy was inaugurated), the United States placed itself at a competitive disadvantage via its domestic price support program. It played the role of a "residual supplier," permitting other countries to market their entire export surpluses (outside of the United States) at prices just below the support price for comparable U.S. grades of cotton. By accumulating huge inventories while acting as the "residual supplier," the United States greatly enhanced the export prospects of competing cotton sellers.[29] Even since 1956, when the United States instituted its export subsidy payments, the CCC has continued to hold substantial inventories, which were as large in 1964 as in 1956.[30]

Table 27

Levels and Long-Term Changes in Cotton Yields for Major Producing and Exporting Countries, 1934-38 and 1961-64

Country	Average Annual Yields in Pounds per Acre 1934-38	1961-65	Percentage Change 1934-38 to 1961-65
United States	212	482	127
Mexico	216	537	149
Peru	439	478	9
Brazil	165	194	18
Syria	159	476	199
Turkey	187	354	89
Sudan	275	308	12
Egypt	478	690	44
India	(90)[a]	118	(33)[a]
Pakistan	(152)[a]	231	(52)[a]
U.S.S.R.	292	606	108
World	180	289	60

Notes: [a]Refers to the period 1948-52, rather than 1934-38, and the gain in yields since then. All raw data are in terms of yield per crop year; 1961-65 data are based on preliminary estimates for the crop year 1964-65.

Source: International Cotton Advisory Committee, Cotton World Statistics, Quarterly Bulletin, April, 1959, pp. 12-41; July, 1962, pp. 8-18; October, 1965, pp. 8-18.

Aside from the United States, India and Pakistan have suffered the greatest losses in the postwar reallocation of the cotton trade. As of the early 1960's, their combined level of cotton production barely exceeded prewar levels, while their level of home consumption has risen dramatically, yielding shrunken export surpluses.[31] Although it is reasonable to allege that the shrunken U.S. export surpluses would probably not have materialized in the absence of persistent government efforts to curtail output, the same cannot be said of

India and Pakistan. In fact, both the Indian and Pakistani Governments have tried to promote cotton production, in the face of well-known difficulties, with the disappointing results shown in Table 26. Only a monumental agricultural development effort on their part would have prevented the rapid erosion of their export surpluses as home consumption grew. It will presently be shown that Mexico's emergence as a major cotton exporter is largely attributable to precisely such a commitment on the part of its government.

Egypt, the last of the prewar triumvirate of major cotton exporters, has experienced a comparatively small decline in its share of the world cotton market. It continues to exploit its competitive advantage based on specialization in long and extra-long staple fibers.

Together, Egypt, India and Pakistan, and the United States accounted for three-fourths or more of the volume of world cotton trade during the 1920's and 1930's. After World War II, they all produced far smaller export surpluses than before and, aided by the rapid postwar recovery of world cotton consumption, thereby triggered an upward price spiral and inventory decumulation on a massive scale.[32]

It was in this sort of international context that Mexico made its successful bid for a major share of the world cotton market. To succeed, the nation's cotton export surplus had to be expanded rapidly. An unusually favorable combination of events, operating from the side of supply, made the latter task a feasible one.

Foremost among the conditions making substantial increases in output possible was the rapid expansion in the amount of suitable land available. As in adjacent parts of the United States, much of the semi-arid land in northern Mexico lacked only a reliable source of water to make it viable for intensive commercial cotton farming operations.[33] The heavy public investments in irrigation projects provided the missing water. As of 1960-61, 85 per cent of the entire cotton crop, by value, was grown on publicly watered land.[34] And 96 per cent of all the cotton, by value, was grown in eight far northern states--the same states that, in 1960-61, accounted for 75 per cent of all the land serviced with publicly produced water.[35]

Aside from providing the indispensable water to the once barren cotton belt, the Mexican Government has been instrumental in providing a number of other essential resources for cotton growers. The foreign trade bank and both the government-owned agricultural banks, for example, have extended substantial amounts of credit to Mexican cotton farmers.[36] The extensive, publicly financed road-building program also facilitated the rapid development of the major cotton growing regions.[37] The government has also acted quite aggressively in assisting domestic growers in their attempts to find foreign buyers for the exportable surplus of cotton, especially in the face of the declining prices and intensified competition witnessed during the late 1950's and early 1960's.[38] Moreover, the land tenure systems that have evolved out of the government-sponsored agrarian reforms have been well suited to the needs of commercial farmers in general, including cotton growers. It is virtually impossible for would-be landed aristocrats to keep large tracts of good land out of production, as was common before the Revolution. Such land is systematically taken over by the government and redistributed. On the other hand, it is possible for a commercial cotton farmer to own legally and work 100 hectares (247 acres) of irrigated land,[39] and larger tracts can be effectively controlled by dispersing legal ownership among members of a family.[40]

The Mexican Government, then, has clearly played a vital and decisive role in conditioning the remarkable sevenfold increase in cotton production since the late 1930's.[41] In addition, various other important and essentially fortuitous circumstances developed after the war that also served to facilitate the rapid expansion of cotton production in Mexico.

In addition to the rapid increase in the available supply of good land (because of the irrigation programs), there has also been a marked improvement, during the postwar period, in the available supply of skilled farm labor. Since World War II, there has been a heavy flow of farm labor from Mexico to the United States and back, under the terms of the various U.S.-Mexican "Bracero" agreements.[42] A recent empirical study confirms the fact that a substantial portion of the "Braceros" acquire skills in the use of farm machinery and become familiar with other aspects of modern U.S. farming methods.[43] It therefore seems reasonable to assume, though data are not available to substantiate it, that many "ex-Braceros" have contributed skilled labor in the rapid expansion of commercial cotton farming in northern Mexico.

Also, even before the war, the giant among the American cotton merchants, Anderson-Clayton & Company, began to move into Mexico and other Latin American countries. Disgruntled with the collapse of the U.S. cotton export business, Will Clayton decided to spread out into promising new producing areas.[44] Mexico was one of the most promising areas to be found. It was nearby, its government was amenable to private foreign investment, and the basic resources needed to expand cotton production were available. Field offices of the company were quickly established all over northern Mexico, providing technical assistance and financing to growers. In return for facilitating the marketing of the growing export surplus, the firm prospered in its customary role as a middleman between domestic growers and foreign buyers.[45]

American farm supply companies also began to move into Mexico by establishing outlets for the sale of their insecticides, seeds, farm implements, fertilizers, and so on.[46] They, too, acted as disseminators of modern technology, thus contributing to the rapid growth of commercial farming in northern Mexico. The fact that mechanized commercial farming has been carried forward most rapidly in the northern region is undoubtedly due, in part, to their presence.[47]

The foregoing discussion produces a picture of a truly impressive constellation of forces contributing to the extremely rapid growth of Mexico's cotton industry during the postwar period. All the basic inputs needed to intensify and expand cotton production were present at a time when world market conditions were propitious. Aside from generating upward of $3 billion in exchange earnings since the war, the development of the cotton industry has contributed to the realization of the nation's broader growth achievements in a number of ways.[48] It has, for example, played a pioneering role in shifting the entire center of gravity in the agriculture sector away from subsistence-oriented corn and bean farming toward modern commercial farming for profit. The high levels of productivity achieved in cotton and other commercial farming operations in northern Mexico have greatly enhanced rural wages in the latter region, even for the _ejidatarios_.[49] Also, more than any other major export item, cotton has permitted Mexico to reduce the geographic polarization of its export trade in the direction of the United States. Most of Mexico's cotton goes to Japan and Europe (though it is largely trans-shipped via the United States).

With the slow but steady decline of world cotton prices in recent years, some of the land and other resources previously committed to the fiber have been shifted toward increasingly attractive alternatives, especially wheat. Once a major import item, wheat has recently begun to appear on the export list and might soon grow in importance there if poor harvests in other major producing areas persist in the face of rising (effective) world demand for the grain.[50] Like cotton, most of Mexico's wheat is grown on publicly watered land in the north of Mexico.[51]

Coffee

On the eve of World War II, Mexico was earning about $6 million per year, as a result of its export effort in coffee.[52] But the entire decade of the 1930's (and the war years, as well) was a trying period for coffee exporters in the sense that prices remained at historically low levels.[53] This unhappy situation was essentially the result of a downturn in the coffee cycle during the early 1930's which was compounded by the combined adverse effects of the Great Depression and the collapse of the European market due to the outbreak of hostilities there.[54] The decade after World War II, on the other hand, was marked by an extremely favorable series of circumstances from the point of view of coffee exporters, including Mexico. The preceding prolonged period of low prices had greatly reduced coffee production and capacity in Brazil, while the Japanese literally destroyed Indonesia's capacity during the war. Brazil, of course, was and is by far the most important producer of all. During the late 1940's, the coffee exporters were unable to meet the sudden sharp recovery in demand, which came with the reopening of the major markets isolated by the war. Prices spiralled upward in a context of massive inventory depletion--causing even Brazil's traditionally unwieldy surplus stocks to disappear temporarily.[55] With the prolonged disaster of the 1930's and early 1940's still fresh in their minds, most coffee producers were even slower than nature requires in responding to the increasingly high prices witnessed in the world market just after the war.[56] Boom conditions therefore spilled over into the early and mid-1950's, while coffee planting finally began to reach a fever pitch, laying the groundwork for the next phase of the coffee cycle. At this point, Mexico's coffee earnings reached their all-time high levels of $100-115 million. Then, when the long delayed supply response finally came, compounded by consumer resistance to the extremely high priced coffee of the mid-1950's, the bottom almost fell out of the coffee market. Prices began to slide downward and the major Latin American producers acted to restrict exports. As the crisis intensified during the late 1950's, a series of increasingly comprehensive agreements were worked out among the producers, culminating in the present agreement, which not only includes virtually all the producing nations, but also enjoys the support of the major importing nations.[57] With the global export quotas set under the present system, coffee prices have lately begun to recover, and Mexico's coffee earnings in 1964 once again approached the $100 million level.

During the swings in the coffee cycle just described, a major reallocation of market shares took place. As Table 28 shows, the Brazilian share of the market has declined precipitously while, almost without exception, other producers have maintained or expanded their market shares since the 1930's.[58] Rowe's study of the world coffee market provides a plausible explanation of the precipitous decline in Brazil's share of the market. Thus, he noted that Brazilian coffee growers have been taxed quite heavily, dampening their incentives to expand capacity during periods of high prices.[59] On the other hand, during periods of low prices, Brazil's coffee retention policies have also been framed so as to bring on a decline in Brazil's share of the market.[60] Moreover, in addition to burning fantastic quantities of coffee during the 1930's, the Brazilians have refrained from attempting to dump their surpluses in more recent years, even though they could undoubtedly successfully undersell the African producers of "robusta" type coffees and regain a larger share of the market in the process.[61] In general, then, Rowe concluded that ". . . Brazil, and to a much lesser extent Colombia, had by themselves to hold up the umbrella of price stabilization while all other producers sheltered under it . . ."[62] He went on to add that the recent International Coffee Agreement has finally firmly committed the other producers to sharing the burden of withholding coffee from the market to shore up prices.

What is of interest here is Mexico's behavior during the

period that Brazil's share of the market was being eroded away. Although African producers have clearly captured most of the market lost by Brazil, Table 28 indicates that Mexico is virtually unique among non-African producers in that it, too, has enlarged its share of the market since the 1930's.

Table 28

Regional Shares of the World Coffee Market, 1929-64
(Volume data are in thousands of metric tons)

World Exports by Volume	1929-33	1934-38	1946-50	1951-55	1956-60	1964
	1,519	1,627	1,840	1,938	2,328	2,813
	Global Percentage Distribution					
Latin America	88.7	85.6	85.7	80.4	73.5	65.4
Brazil	60.5	55.1	53.6	44.8	40.3	31.9
Colombia	12.6	14.6	17.3	17.4	14.3	13.7
Mexico	2.0	2.3	2.1	3.4	3.4	3.8
Africa	4.8	8.0	13.4	17.8	23.7	30.8
Asia and Oceania	6.5	6.4	.9	2.2	2.3	3.8

Note: Columns may not total to 100 due to rounding.

Sources: 1964: Pan American Coffee Bureau, Annual Coffee Statistics (New York: Pan American Coffee Bureau), No. 28, 1964, pp. 56-57; 1929-1960: FAO, The World Coffee Economy (Rome: FAO, 1961), pp. 57-58.

Given that the total volume of coffee moving in world commerce has expanded by about 50 per cent since the 1930's, Mexico has had to generate a substantially larger export surplus of coffee over the period in question to achieve its modest penetration of the coffee market. The latter feat was accomplished by a doubling of coffee production between 1950 and 1963.[63] Unlike the experience in cotton, however, it cannot be said that the government has made an all-out effort to facilitate and encourage a rapid expansion of coffee production. Rather, most Mexican coffee is grown in regions of the country that have not received much attention until quite recently, insofar as the various relevant public spending programs are concerned (for example, road building and irrigation).[64] Moreover, the government has lately acted to take land out of coffee and shift it to rubber, in hopes of eventually driving the latter item off the import list.[65] On the other hand, the Agriculture Department has provided loans and substantial technical assistance to coffee growers in an attempt to raise coffee yields on land already committed to the crop.[66] On the latter point, it should be noted that in addition to enjoying the marketing advantages accruing to sellers of mild "arabica" type coffees, the Mexican growers are relatively low-cost producers, experiencing higher average yields than most of their competitors.[67]

In light of the foregoing discussion, the following prediction of the Combined Mexican Working Party, made in 1952, seems particularly incisive:

> Since October 1949, however, an estimated two million coffee trees have been planted in Mexico and production from these trees should be felt in the next year or two. . . . However, most other producing countries are also believed to be planting trees, and if this is so, the increased supplies will eventually affect prices. Should this occur, higher Mexican production may offset some of the reduction in earnings due to a fall in price.[68]

And that is precisely what happened.

Finally, since the coffee industry is centered in one of the poorest parts of the country, its expansion has served to offset, to a limited extent, the regional income disparities discussed in Chapter 2. It differs in this respect from the cotton and tourist industries, which have served to make the relatively rich areas even richer.

Sugar

Immediately before and during World War II, Mexico typically imported sugar.[69] By the end of the Korean War, the need for imports had clearly been eliminated. Since 1960, upward of $50 million per year have been earned via sugar exports. As a result of these developments, sugar has become one of Mexico's major merchandise exports.[70]

Mexico's achievement of the status of a sugar surplus

nation was made possible via a truly remarkable expansion of home production, comparable in fact to the extraordinary rise in the quantum of cotton production discussed earlier. As Table 29 shows, sugar production has increased roughly five-fold since World War II, more than matching the rapid expansion in home consumption. Much of this very large increment in output has come about as a result of an extension in the amount of land planted to cane, a development facilitated by various public investment programs.[71] There has, for example, been a sizable increase in the amount of cane grown on irrigated land. By 1960, about one-third of the crop, by value, was grown on publicly watered land.[72] Aside from the expansion onto irrigated land, however, government-financed flood control projects in the southeastern part of the country have permitted a substantial extension of the area planted to cane in the rich alluvial soils of the river valleys there.[73] The latter region, in and around Vera Cruz, is the traditional center of the sugar industry.[74]

Table 29

Mexico's Production, Consumption, and Exports of Sugar, 1940-64
(Thousands of metric tons at raw values)

				Exports		
Year	Production	Home Consumption	End of Year Stocks	Total	to U.S. Only	U.S. Quota
1940	296	363	15	0	0	
1945	369	452	53	0	0	
1950	618	584	60	20	6	
1955	961	871	250	80	12	
1958	1,210	1,015	250	187	65	
1959	1,448	1,061	503	135	63	64
1960	1,518	1,118	440	462	382	400
1961	1,488	1,116	164	612	611	685
1962	1,531	1,246	99	350	350	410
1963	1,756	1,318	130	377	343	387
1964	1,931	1,424	117	486	425	479

Source: International Sugar Council, Sugar Yearbook, various issues.

As of the mid-1950's, then, the domestic carry-over of sugar had been built up substantially. (See Table 29.) The Mexican sugar producers' association, backed by various government agencies, began to search aggressively for ways and means of penetrating existing foreign markets on a much larger scale.[75] The latter task, however, turned out to be a frustrating and formidable one, because of the nature of the then extant institutional arrangements in the world market.

Because of its immense size and immediate proximity, the U.S. market, of course, constituted the logical outlet for Mexico's surplus sugar. Aside from its location, the U.S. market offered the added attraction of prices which, even net of duties, were typically well above the so-called world market price.[76] But entry into the U.S. market had long been restricted via a rigid quota system, and frequent pleas of the Mexican Government for a larger quota were long ignored.

Other major segments of the world sugar market were also blocked off via various special arrangements among particular sets of countries. The British and Canadian markets have, in the main, been reserved for sugar surplus countries within the British Commonwealth.[77] Various other European countries maintain preferential arrangements with the sugar exporters among their present and former dependencies.[78] Mexico, of course, has not qualified for membership in such cliques.

Finally, what remains of the "world sugar market" net of these special arrangements has also been apportioned out among the sugar surplus countries--under the terms of the International Sugar Agreement (ISA), operative from 1953 to the present, except for a lapse from 1962-65. It is the price at which sugar moves under the ISA quotas that is usually referred to as the "world market price." It is normally lower than the U.S. price, net of duties, and lower than the special prices arranged within the British Commonwealth Sugar Agreement.[79]

As an ardent protagonist of international commodity agreements, the Mexican Government would not permit its sugar growers to operate outside the ISA. Rather, during the late 1950's, repeated attempts were made to have the 75,000-ton Mexican allotment at least doubled, but without success.[80] Thus, in spite of their proven ability to generate a sizable sugar surplus,[81] the Mexicans found themselves boxed in by a maze of quotas basically reflecting glut conditions in the world sugar market.

Then, in the year 1959-60, Mexico's fortunes as a sugar seller improved dramatically and suddenly, as a direct result of the Cuban Crisis.[82] Between 1959 and 1960, Mexico's allotment under the U.S. quota system was increased from less than 100,000 to 400,000 tons.[83] Virtually all of Mexico's surplus sugar has gone to the U.S. since then, but the quota has not quite been filled.

Other Agricultural Exports

Cotton, coffee, and sugar clearly stand out as Mexico's most noteworthy agricultural exports. They are all important items individually in the sense that they have each brought in over $50 million per year, on the average, since 1960. Moreover, they have collectively invariably accounted for upward of 30 per cent of all merchandise export earnings since 1955. (See Figure 1.) Nonetheless, they by no means exhaust the list of agricultural commodities that consistently appear among Mexico's merchandise exports. There are, for example, a variety of fruits and vegetables grown in north and north-central Mexico that essentially supplement the domestic U.S. (and in some cases Canadian) supplies of such commodities. In some cases, they enjoy the marketing advantage of reaching maturity before the comparable U.S. crops. Most important among the latter group of items are tomatoes, watermelons, cantaloupes, citrus fruits, and strawberries.[84] Though only the tomatoes have lately accounted for as much as $20 million per year in exchange earnings, a number of factors now operative in the U.S. fruit and vegetable industries may soon provide a sharp stimulus to Mexican exports of such products. Specifically, the termination of the "Bracero" program, together with other potent reform measures explicitly designed to raise agricultural wages on farms in the United States, may just drive the prices of such commodities upward by raising the costs of U.S. growers. Mexican suppliers may then find themselves in an increasingly favorable competitive position vis-à-vis U.S. growers, for obvious reasons.

Finally, a by-product of Mexico's impressive achievement

of self-sufficiency in food grains has been the intermittent appearance of wheat and corn on the export list. Though neither of these products has become firmly established as an industry consistently providing a substantial export surplus, both have, on occasion, generated sizable exchange earnings in particular recent years.[85] If a persistent wheat shortage should develop in the world market, bringing historically high prices with it, Mexico is in an excellent position to react quickly by taking irrigated land out of cotton.

Meat Exports

Since 1960, Mexico has been earning roughly $50 million per annum via exports of cattle on the hoof and as fresh or frozen carcasses.[86] Beef animals account for essentially all the cattle and carcasses exported. With the exception of very small-scale shipments to other parts of Latin America and to Europe, virtually all Mexico's meat goes to the U.S. market.

Compared with earnings realized during the 1930's and 1940's (or any earlier period), the levels recently achieved represent a substantial gain over past performances. The highest level of earnings generated during the 1940's, for example, was $10 million in 1943.[87]

In spite of the impressive gains just cited, most studies of the Mexican livestock industry concur in the finding that its performance during most of the postwar period has left much to be desired. Whereas other major beef surplus nations have often found demand conditions and commercial policies in the advanced countries the main barrier restricting growth of their export business, there is abundant evidence available to indicate that Mexico could readily have earned much more via beef exports through much of the postwar period, even without going beyond the U.S. market.

To begin with, between 1947 and 1952, and again between 1953 and 1954, Mexico was unable to export any beef (on the hoof) to the United States, because of a widespread epidemic of hoof-and-mouth disease. Though isolated cases of this disease occur occasionally, even in the United States, it cannot assume endemic dimensions where modern techniques of cattle inspection and control are applied. Various other (only slightly less costly) diseases have also limited cattle production in Mexico during much of the postwar period.[88]

A more fundamental supply problem, however, concerns the general absence of modern techniques for breeding, feeding, and marketing cattle. As of the late 1950's, an FAO study found the Mexican cattle industry deficient on all three counts.[89] Finally, the simple fact that the Mexican Government at times has directly limited cattle exports via an export quota system also lends credence to the notion that more could have been made of the opportunities available during the 1940's and 1950's if more high quality beef had been produced.[90]

Since 1960 or so, however, both private cattlemen and the government have shown an appreciation of the problems and have made decisive moves to correct them. Mexican cattlemen now have a lively interest in developing registered herds of purebred cattle, as witnessed by their sizable imports of breeding stock from the United States.[91] Modern methods of intensive feeding have also become more common, and the government has fostered the development of a network of feedlots designed to produce high-grade fattened cattle for export.[92] A variety of other measures, especially in the field of meat inspection and grading, have been instituted to foster the growth of the cattle export industry.[93] With these measures, the supply limitations to Mexico's performance as a meat exporter may eventually become less important, and Mexico's earnings on this account might continue to rise.[94]

Finally, since cattle for export are raised in various parts of the country, the regional impact of the industry cannot be said to have promoted the geographical pattern of income inequalities discussed in Chapter 2. It is true, however, that most of the meat processing establishments for handling carcasses destined for export are located in the far northern part of the country.

Seafood Exports

Prior to 1945, Mexico never earned as much as $5 million per year via exports of seafood.[95] During the postwar period, however, seafood export earnings gradually rose toward their current levels, generating about $50 million per year.[96] Shrimp is by far the most important seafood export, accounting for roughly 90 per cent of earnings as of the early 1960's.[97] Virtually the entire export surplus has been sold in the United States.[98]

The primary stimulus for the rapid growth of Mexican seafood exports came via the prodigious postwar expansion of the U.S. market for frozen shrimp. Between 1939 and 1955, U.S. shrimp consumption per capita more than doubled, and consumption has continued to rise, though at a more modest pace, since then.[99] The latter phenomenon is largely attributable to postwar technological innovations in the processing, packaging, and distribution of shrimp. Specifically, the process of quick-freezing fresh foods for nationwide distribution (to commercial users and households) was first applied to shrimp on a large scale during the late 1940's, and an economically viable method of breading frozen shrimp was developed.[100] Consumer acceptance of the product exceeded the expectations of distributors, and severe shortages of the raw material were reported in trade magazines during the early 1950's.[101] Even in a context of steadily improved prices at the wholesale level, the U.S. shrimp fleets were unable to meet the rapidly rising demand for their product, providing a highly favorable situation for the small but expanding Mexican shrimp fleets.[102]

The initial Mexican reaction on the supply side occurred in the Gulf Coastal region adjacent to the Campeche Bank, a traditional trawling ground for the U.S. fleet. Freezing plants were quickly established in the area to facilitate handling of the product. The boom conditions in the shrimp industry in the state of Campeche did much to improve levels of living in that relatively underdeveloped region. Soon, however, the focal point of production shifted to the far northwest, mainly in the Bay of California.[103] The latter area enjoyed the advantage of being closer to major U.S. distribution centers and relatively free of competition from U.S. shrimp fleets.[104] Further investments were undertaken in packing and freezing facilities there, with encouragement from the government's Foreign Trade Bank. As of the early 1960's, the greatest part of Mexico's shrimp catch was landed in the states of Sinaloa and Sonora--two of the richest states in Mexico.[105]

As the U.S. market expanded, the landings of the U.S. shrimp fleets came to represent a distinctly smaller share of the total U.S. supply, with foreign suppliers gaining a substantial share of the growing U.S. market, as shown in Table 30. Mexico was the first important foreign supplier, accounting for virtually all U.S. imports as of the mid-1950's. Since then, various other underdeveloped countries have joined Mexico in providing shrimp for the U.S. market, as shown in

Table 30

Total Supply of Shrimp in the U.S. Market, by Source, 1950-63[a]
(Millions of pounds of "heads-off, shells-on" shrimp)

Year	Total Domestic Landings (1)	Total Imports[a] (2)	Imports from Mexico Only[a] (3)	Total U.S. Shrimp Supply[b] (1) + (2) (4)	Col. (2) ÷ Col. (4) (5)	Col. (3) ÷ Col. (2) (6)
1950	114	40	40	154	26	99
1955	145	54	45	199	27	83
1956	133	67	54	200	34	81
1957	121	70	48	191	37	69
1958	128	85	56	205	41	66
1959	143	107	69	250	42	64
1960	149	113	74	262	43	65
1961	104	134	79	238	56	59
1962	119	153	77	272	56	50
1963	150	167	78	317	53	47

Notes: All figures rounded to the nearest integer.
[a]Import data reported in the sources named below are taken from U.S. Bureau of the Census, *Foreign Trade Reports* (Series FT110).
[b]Gross of exports, which usually account for well under 10 per cent of Column (4).

Sources: 1950-60: U.S. Tariff Commission, *Report on Investigation No. 332-40: Shrimp* (Washington, D.C.: U.S. Government Printing Office, March, 1961), pp. 149-156; 1961-63: U.S. Bureau of Commercial Fisheries, *Commercial Fisheries Review*, June, 1964, p. 27.

Table 30, thereby reducing Mexico's share of U.S. imports.[106] Nonetheless, the value of Mexico's shrimp earnings has continued to expand at a modest pace over the past decade. Prospects for the industry are promising, since U.S. per capita shrimp consumption has continued to rise.

In shrimp, then, as in the case of the tourist industry, the Mexicans again clearly demonstrated their ability to capitalize on a promising export opportunity in the adjacent U.S. market. Also, as in the case of other export industries, the government has lent meaningful and tangible support to the industry in various ways. It has, for example, expanded facilities for training shrimp fishermen in the use of modern techniques for finding and exploiting shrimp feeding grounds.[107] It has also extended credit to the industry and protected the nine-mile limit against incursions of U.S. shrimp fleets.[108] In defending its negative opinion on a recent U.S. Senate proposal to apply a heavy tariff on shrimp imports, the U.S. Tariff Commission cited the fact that many of the best shrimping grounds in the Bay of California and the Gulf of Mexico fall within the Mexican nine-mile limit and could, therefore, not be exploited by the U.S. fleet.[109]

Mineral Exports

The Major Metal Exports

In light of Mexico's economic history, it seems ironic that seafood should turn out to be a more important source of foreign exchange than any of the metals that, for decades, were the mainstays of the export sector of the economy. Figure 1 shows that copper, lead, zinc, gold, and silver accounted for roughly three-fifths of export earnings in 1940. As of 1963 and 1964, however, seafood brought in more dollars than gold and silver, or copper and lead, or zinc. As a group, these metals account for only about one-sixth of export earnings. Since they are now relatively unimportant export industries individually and are closely related from the side of supply, they will be analyzed here in two sub-groups.[110] The first group consists of the major industrial metals produced for foreign markets: copper, lead, and zinc.

Copper, Lead, and Zinc. Table 6 showed that the mining sector in the Mexican economy expanded less rapidly than any other major sector between 1940 and 1963. The major export-oriented metal producing industries have contributed disproportionately to that performance, especially since the late 1950's. The absolute volume of copper, lead, and zinc produced and exported has apparently actually declined while home consumption of each of these metals has increased sharply, as may be seen in Tables 31 and 32. A detailed analysis of world market conditions for each of the metals in question will not be presented here, but a few general observations are in order on the external economic aspects of Mexico's recent mediocre performance as an exporter of these products.[111]

Table 31

Mexico's Production and Home Consumption of Copper, Lead, and Zinc, 1939-64 (Thousands of metric tons per year)

	1939-41	1950-53	1955	1957	1960	1963	1964
Copper							
Production	43	62	55	61	61	56	53
Consumption	--	11	18	19	24	36	36
Lead							
Production	190	233	211	214	192	190	175
Consumption	--	11	22	34	35	68	75
Zinc							
Production	134	214	269	243	268	240	236
Consumption	--	13	15	19	28	31	40

Notes: All the above data refer to recovered metal or (roughly) estimated metal content of ores. Consumption data are rough estimates compiled by the American Bureau of Metal Statistics, as cited below. All figures are rounded.

-- indicates that relevant data are not available.

Sources: Production Data: Nacional Financiera, 50 años de Revolución Mexicana en cifras (México: Talleres Gráficos Nacionales, 1963), p. 64; Banco Nacional de Comercio Exterior, Comercio Exterior de México, monthly edition in Spanish, March, 1965, p. 250; Consumption Data: American Bureau of Metal Statistics, Yearbook, 1964 and 1955.

Table 32

World Prices and Mexican Exports of Copper, Lead, and Zinc, 1939-64[a]
(Exports in thousands of metric tons per year; prices in U.S. cents per pound; values in millions of dollars)

	1939-41	1945-47	1950-53	1955	1957	1960	1963	1964
Copper								
Exports	44	56	78	80	62	37	25	18
World Price[b]	11.3	15.5	24.6	37.5	29.6	32.0	30.6	32.0
Value	9	15	25[e]	67	37	26	22	14
Lead								
Exports	178	179	222	170	169	145	137	105
World Price[c]	5.3	8.4	15.2	15.1	14.7	11.9	11.1	13.6
Value	16	31	70[e]	53	51	34	27	22
Zinc								
Exports	131	187	339	419	395	409	384	347
World Price[d]	6.3	9.1	14.73	12.3	11.4	12.9	12.0	13.6
Value	7	20	25[e]	28	36	29	30	36

Notes to Table 32

Notes: [a]These data are not precisely comparable to those of the previous table, because the volume figures do not accurately reflect metal content of exports. Instead, the export volume data simply report tons of ore, concentrates, or semi-finished metal shipped. In the case of zinc, the greater part of the export bundle is in the form of concentrates, whereas most of the copper and lead shipped abroad are in metallic form.

[b]Average spot price of electrolytic copper at New York.

[c]Average spot price of pig lead at New York.

[d]Average spot price of prime slab zinc at East St. Louis.

[e]1950 only.

Sources: Prices: American Bureau of Metal Statistics, Yearbook, 1964, p. 140.

Export Volume Data: Banco de México, Informe(s) Anual(es), 1960-64; Banco Nacional de Comercio Exterior, Comercio Exterior de México (Yearbook), 1954, pp. 163-72; Banco de México, Riqueza Mineria y Yacamientos Minerales de México (México, D. F.: Talleres Nacionales, 1956), pp. 93, 147, 161; Comercio Exterior, monthly in English, April, 1957, p. 23; April, 1958, p. 24.

Export Value Data: Table 43.

Although the global consumption of copper, lead, and zinc has increased substantially since World War II, as shown in Table 33, the total value of trade in such metals has been quite sensitive to changes in the levels of industrial production in the advanced countries.[112] Also, the cyclical behavior of prices of these metals has been rather unstable relative to price changes for primary products in general.[113]

Table 33

World Consumption and U.S. Imports of Copper, Lead, and Zinc, 1947-64

A. Estimated Free World Consumption of Copper, Lead, Zinc (Millions of tons)

	1947	1954	1960	1964
Copper	2.55	3.04	4.11	4.92
Lead	1.47	1.88	1.97	2.31
Zinc	1.67	2.15	2.63	3.37

B. U.S. Imports of Copper, Lead, Zinc[a] (Including metal content of ores and concentrates; thousands of long tons)

	Copper	Lead[b]	Zinc[c]
1947	414 (76)	212 (90)	370 (164)
1950	696 (63)	522 (223)	434 (177)
1952	619 (51)	616 (201)	565 (219)
1954-58 (average)	575 (50)	487 (94)	702 (200)
1960	525 (22)	352 (72)	577 (198)
1962	583 (24)	401 (70)	609 (177)
1964	583 (13)	336 (74)	475 (117)

Notes: [a]Figures in parentheses show imports from Mexico only.
[b]Excludes inconsequential imports of scrap containing lead and lead in type metal.
[c]Excludes minor imports of zinc dust.

Sources: American Bureau of Metal Statistics, Yearbook (various years); U.S. Bureau of Mines, Mineral Facts and Problems, 1965.

But perhaps the most important developments in the world markets for these metals from Mexico's point of view have been the changing conditions in the U. S. market. Owing to its size and proximity, it has long absorbed the largest part of Mexico's metal surpluses. Part B of Table 33 shows postwar trends in U. S. imports of copper, lead, and zinc. The figures in parentheses represent imports from Mexico.

During the early postwar period, then, world consumption of copper, lead, and zinc expanded rapidly in a context of rising prices. U. S. import requirements for copper, lead, and zinc (including "needs" for strategic stockpiling purposes) also expanded rapidly. Under the impact of these potent demand side stimuli, the volume and value of Mexican exports advanced sharply, as shown in Table 32.

But world market conditions began to deteriorate in the middle and late 1950's. Prices weakened first for lead and zinc, then for copper. A series of policy decisions taken in the United States impaired Mexico's chances of expanding its exports of these metals. First of all, the U. S. Government sharply reduced its purchases of these and other metals for the strategic reserve stockpile.[114] Copper import duties, after being suspended in 1951, were reimposed in July of 1958.[115] Direct subsidies were granted to small, high-cost domestic lead and zinc producers whenever prices reached historically low levels. Copper, lead, and zinc producers also received heavy subsidies to defray the costs of seeking new ore bodies.[116] Finally, and most important of all, an outright import quota was established for lead and zinc late in 1958. This quota arrangement remained in force through 1965 and was discontinued in 1966. In a context of declining world prices and a contrived shrinkage of the U. S. market, only an extraordinary effort to cut costs and increase output, while competing aggressively in other segments of the world market, would have enabled the Mexicans to expand their exchange earnings via the export of such metals. No such effort was made.

It is quite clear that uneasy relations between the government and the large foreign-owned mining companies, together with a continued depletion of high-grade ore reserves, combined to compound the difficulties caused by the adverse external economic conditions.[117] These factors are closely related and have been the subject of much heated debate within the country. Although essentially amiable working relationships have been established between the government and foreign investors interested in participating in so-called new and necessary [manufacturing] industries, there is far less rapport with regard to the mining interests of foreigners. Mexicans are extremely sensitive about the exploitation of their nonrenewable resources, and an uneasy truce has been maintained with the foreign companies ever since the oil industry was nationalized in 1938. The special tax concessions granted to new foreign investment in many manufacturing industries do not apply to mining. Even in the face of sharp declines in world prices, heavy export taxes have been maintained on metal exports with differentially high rates being applied to unprocessed ores as compared to exports of concentrates or pure metal.[118] This, of course, places the exporters in an awkward position, since the advanced countries typically levy differentially high <u>import</u> duties on processed metals vis-à-vis unprocessed ores.[119] Moreover, the rate at which the export duty is assessed is geared to increase directly with the world market price of each metal, thereby reducing the much needed incentive effect of rising prices.

Finally, the investment policies of foreign-owned mining companies have undoubtedly served to intensify supply difficulties in the industry. In Chapter 2, it was noted that very little of the recent capital inflow on private account has been directed toward the mining sector.[120] In light of the uncertainty facing the foreign companies, this seems understandable from their point of view, inasmuch as they have ample alternative opportunities to develop new sources of these raw materials in other countries (for example, Canada). But their failure to modernize their operations in Mexico and to search out new ore bodies has only heightened the government's inclination to ease them out of the country. In the 1960's, pressures on the large foreign companies have been intensified, causing some of them to sell their controlling interests in a number of the largest mining operations in Mexico.[121]

<u>Silver and Gold</u>. From the demand side, the world market situations for gold and silver have developed in a peculiar manner, because of certain aspects of the behavior of the U.S. Government. Since 1935, the demand for gold in the world market has been perfectly elastic at a fixed price of $35.00 per fine ounce. That price is, of course, the rate at which the U.S. Government buys gold (and sells it to industrial

consumers).

The world market price of silver, on the other hand, currently stands at about three times its immediate prewar level. (See Table 34.) The causes of this profound rise in the price of silver may be summarized briefly as follows.[122] In recent decades, the demand for silver for monetary and nonmonetary purposes (especially the latter) has increased rapidly. On the other hand, both in Mexico and the United States, the most important producing countries, known reserves of high-grade ores and the native metal have been gradually depleted.[123] An increasing proportion of new production has come about as a by-product of the mining of other metals. After the Korean War, the demand for silver exceeded available new supplies at a world market "ceiling price" effectively determined by U.S. Treasury silver sales policy. Between 1946 and 1961, the U.S. Treasury was authorized to sell silver to industrial users at $.91 per ounce. By 1961, depletion of the Treasury's silver stocks led to the suspension of such sales. With the closing down of that source of supply, prices advanced further, reaching a level of $1.29 per ounce in 1964.

Given these conditions in the world markets for gold and silver, it is interesting to examine Mexico's behavior as a supplier and its related export earnings. In the face of a rigidly fixed world price and a steady depletion of reserves of high-grade ores, it is not surprising to find that gold production has declined sharply since 1940.

The same thing has happened in many other gold producing nations, with the significant exception of the most important producer, South Africa.[124] Aside from the problem of depletion of reserves, the institutional problems mentioned in the discussion of copper, lead, and zinc have also had a detrimental effect here, since the important companies producing those metals are also major gold producers. Moreover, the Mexican Government levies the same set of taxes, including export duties, on gold and silver producers as are levied on producers of lead, copper, and zinc.

Though far less pronounced than in the case of gold, silver production has also declined during the recent period of rapid growth, as shown in Table 34. Since it is now mainly produced from lean ores, and as a joint product with copper and/or lead and/or zinc, it is not too surprising to find that

Table 34

Domestic Production and the Value of Mexico's Gold and Silver Exports, 1939-64

	1939-41	1950-53	1955	1957	1960	1963	1964
Estimated value of nonmonetary gold and silver exports	60	53	48	57	48	51	45
Silver production (million fine ounces)	81.1	47.8	48.0	47.1	44.5	42.8	41.7
World price of silver	36.3	86.2	89.1	90.8	91.4	127.9	129.3
Gold production (thousand fine ounces	842	427	383	346	300	238	210

Notes: Value data are in millions of dollars. The "world price" of silver is the average spot price per fine ounce in New York, in U.S. cents.

Production data do not include the gold content of various industrial metal ores and concentrates shipped abroad. However, the total value of (nonmonetary) gold and silver exports shown in the top line of this table does include a crude estimate of the value of the recoverable gold and silver in such ores. No reliable and consistent quantum index of gold and silver exports covering the period in question here is available.

Sources: Banco de México, Riqueza Minera y Yacamientos Minerales de México (México, D. F.: Talleres Nacionales, 1956), pp. 92, 118. American Bureau of Metal Statistics, Yearbook, 1964 and 1955; Table 43.

output declined during periods when market conditions for the latter products were unfavorable, for example, in the late 1950's. But during the early 1960's, the world market prices of copper, lead, zinc, and silver all showed some improvement. Yet the output of such products has thus far failed to respond to the stimulus of higher prices. Moreover, the U.S. import quotas for lead and zinc were lifted early in 1966. If the prices of these metals continue to improve and production and exports do not soon increase, it will be abundantly clear that Mexico's mediocre performance as an exporter of metals has deep supply roots in addition to the more widely discussed demand difficulties.

Besides encouraging the "Mexicanization" of these mining industries, the government has recently announced a broad frontal assault on the resource depletion and productivity problems in the mining sector. Aside from the tax reductions for the companies that are no longer foreign controlled, the reform involves an extension of government credit and subsidies designed to help domestic producers discover new sources of raw materials and apply modern recovery techniques, and so on.[125] Only time will tell how the program will work out.

Other Mineral Exports

Mexico regularly exports small amounts of various other minerals, including manganese, mercury, fluorspar, and barium sulphate. Although they are not important enough to warrant special attention here, it is worth noting that such minerals together brought in a bit more than $20 million in 1963 and 1964, accounting for about 2 per cent of merchandise export earnings in the process. Two rather important nonmetal mineral exports, however, do merit special attention: sulfur and petroleum.

Sulfur. Sulfur provides the only significant exception to the recent generally mediocre export performances of Mexico's mining industries. Before the Korean War, Mexican production and exports of sulfur were inconsequential, barely satisfying growing domestic needs. Since then, as shown in Table 35, output and foreign sales have both expanded very rapidly. In the process, Mexico has risen to its present position as the world's second ranking sulfur producer (behind the United States). The spectacular increase in Mexican sulfur production and exports came about as a direct result of

U.S. Export-Import Bank loans to two (U.S. controlled) companies, which discovered extensive deposits of elemental sulfur in one of the poorest and least developed regions of Mexico, the Isthmus of Tehuantepec.[126]

Table 35

Mexico's Production and Exports of Sulfur, 1950-64

	1950	1955	1960	1961	1962	1963	1964
Production[a]	13	521	1,331	1,246	1,448	1,544	1,733
Export volume[a]	--	180	1,254	1,154	1,331	1,507	1,841
Export value[b]	--	5	28	29	30	34	38

Notes: [a]In thousands of metric tons.
[b]In millions of dollars.
--Indicates insignificant amounts.

Sources: The value data are from Table 42. Production and export volume data are from Comercio Exterior, monthly English edition, June, 1965, p. 2, and various issues of Banco de Mexico, Informe Anual.

A chronic shortage of sulfur was witnessed in the world market throughout the 1940's.[127] World consumption of elemental sulfur exceeded production in a context of rising prices and inventory depletion after World War II, with a particularly severe shortage occurring during the Korean crisis, just before the Mexican deposits were discovered. The foreign-owned companies have expanded output and exports so rapidly since then that the Mexican Government has found it advisable to restrict sulfur exports on the grounds that Mexico will need its sulfur to meet rising home consumption in the future.[128]

Further discoveries of sulfur deposits in Canada and France temporarily lowered the "posted prices" of the major international companies during the late 1950's. Nonetheless, the long-term outlook for sulfur surplus nations is quite favorable from the side of demand, since the need for sulfur in both its agricultural and industrial uses is growing rapidly.[129]

Petroleum. Writing in the early 1950's, members of the Combined Mexican Working Party found that Mexico, the country that inaugurated the world's oil bonanza, ". . . faces the prospect of a diminishing export surplus of petroleum in the immediate future and a deficit after a few years."[130] This prediction was based on a projected rapid rise in home consumption, coupled with a continued depletion of known reserves and difficultues in financing extensive and expensive exploratory drilling.

The truly oil-rich countries have lately had to concern themselves primarily with the problem of finding markets for their huge export surpluses, but Mexico's problems as an oil exporter have, by and large, been supply problems.[131] On the twentieth anniversary of the nationalization of the petroleum industry in 1958, the director of the government oil monopoly (Petroleos Mexicanos, or PEMEX) noted that an all-out effort would have to be made to keep oil off the import list.[132] As of 1965, the new director of PEMEX, with 21 per cent of the Federal Budget at his disposal, still reported that PEMEX was barely able to keep abreast of the rapid increase in home consumption of petroleum products.[133]

Table 36 summarizes the trends since 1940 in the production and exports of petroleum and natural gas. All of the natural gas crosses the U.S. border via pipeline to a few local markets, and most of the petroleum (mainly residual fuel oils) also goes to the United States. Barring the discovery of major new fields, Mexico will be unlikely to produce a much larger export surplus in the near future.

The major oil fields currently exploited are all along the eastern seaboard of the nation, and, as of 1962, about one-third of the crude oil and gas produced by PEMEX came from the relatively poor region around the Isthmus of Tehuantepec. Vera Cruz and Tamaulipas, two moderately well-to-do states, account for the greatest part of oil and gas production.[134] However, in locating its refineries and product distribution centers, PEMEX has explicitly attempted to avoid aggravating regional inequalities in levels of income and economic development. Thus, where feasible, new refineries have been built in relatively poor areas.

Table 36

Mexico's Production and Exports of Petroleum and Natural Gas, 1940-64

	1940	1950	1955	1960	1963	1964
Production (volume)[a]						
Petroleum	44	74	92	109	126	135
Natural gas	1.05	1.76	3.39	9.66	11.4	13.3
Exports (volume)[a]						
Petroleum	19	24	29	15	19	19
Natural gas	--	--	--	1.39	1.34	1.69
Value of exports of petroleum and gas[b]	17	32	50	20	37	38

Notes: [a]Production and export volume data are in millions of standard barrels and billions of cubic meters for petroleum and gas, respectively.

[b]Value data are in millions of dollars. Petroleum production data refer to crude oil only, while the export data refer to the combined volume of crude and refined products exported.

-- indicates insignificant quantities.

Sources: Report of the Combined Mexican Working Party, The Economic Development of Mexico (Baltimore: Johns Hopkins Press, 1953), pp. 258-60; also Tables 41 and 42 and sources cited therein.

Other Exports

The industries discussed in detail above have typically accounted for well over two-thirds of Mexico's merchandise export earnings since World War II.[135] Moreover, combined with estimated earnings from the border and tourist trade, they account, as of the mid-1960's, for roughly three-fourths of all earned foreign exchange. There is, however, a substantial residual of export earnings.

A number of relatively minor but well established agricultural and mineral export industries collectively account for a sizable slice of the residual. A few such industries were mentioned in passing above.[136] Also, the two most important food grains produced in the agricultural sector, maize and wheat, occasionally generate a substantial export income, thereby, on the average, accounting for another small part of the residual.[137]

Finally, there is a small but intriguing part of the export bundle consisting of "manufactured goods." Of course, most of the agricultural and mineral exports already discussed are, in a very real sense, "manufactured goods." For example, virtually all of Mexico's cotton is now ginned and packed (baled) before being shipped abroad.[138] Furthermore, though essentially all the coffee leaving the country is in the form of sacked beans, at least a small portion of the sugar is refined, and exports of molasses usually bring in a few million dollars. Also, much of the shrimp annually exported is decapitated, shelled, deveined, frozen (or iced), and packed within Mexico. By value, almost all of the lead, copper, gold, and silver leaving the country is in the form of refined metal, although zinc exports are still mainly in the form of ores and concentrates. Virtually all the sulfur exported is in the semi-processed state of elemental sulfur, since it is mined via the Frasch process. Henequen fiber, once a major crude fiber export, now brings in roughly $25 million per year when shipped in the form of simple manufactured goods (mainly binder twine), though the raw fiber is also still exported on a modest scale.[139] Finally, close to half of the meat exported in recent years (by value) has been slaughtered and subjected to some processing within Mexico.[140]

Yates' detailed study of the geographic distribution of manufacturing activities within Mexico showed that the various types of export-oriented manufacturing activity just discussed (together with petroleum processing and the textile industry) provided for virtually all value added in manufacturing outside of the immediate environs of the Federal District and Monterrey. In other words, manufacturing concerns which add value to primary products destined for export account for much of the very limited decentralization of manufacturing witnessed to date, and the greatest part of this processing of goods for export occurs in the far northern reaches of the country, helping to generate and maintain differentially high incomes there.[141] The reasons for this concentration of export processing activities are fairly obvious. Many of the most important primary products produced for export come from precisely that region. Also, well over half the export bundle, by value, leaves the country via overland routes to the United States.[142]

Aside from adding some value to most of its primary product exports, Mexico also sells a very small but growing bundle of more highly fabricated goods in foreign markets. Items, that is, which appear in the Standard International Trade Classification (SITC) with numbers in the five, six, seven, and eight hundreds, but not including those already discussed, especially processed nonferrous metals (group number 680).[143]

Beginning with the SITC 500 group of products (chemicals), only two items of any significance have appeared among Mexico's exports under this heading in recent years--lead oxides, used in paints, and natural hormones. As of 1960-63, chemicals accounted for about 3 per cent of export earnings. Aside from the processed metals already mentioned, only modest amounts of textiles (mainly yarn and thread), and simple iron and steel shapes appear among the SITC 600 group of items, labeled "manufactured goods classified by material." Between 1960 and 1963, exports of "machinery and transport equipment" (SITC 700) never exceeded $10 million in value, while exports of "other manufactured articles" (SITC 800) brought in less than $20 million.[144] Virtually everything else of any significance in the SITC classification of Mexico's exports was covered in previous sections of this chapter.[145]

It is clear, therefore, that Mexico still depends on exports of "primary products" (albeit processed ones) for virtually all of its merchandise export income.[146] But, as in most other developing countries, the Mexican Government is actively interested in (and engaged in) promoting exports of manufactured goods.[147] However, even if the barriers to entry of such goods in advanced countries' markets were removed, it is not at all clear that most of Mexico's established manufacturing industries could as yet compete successfully. Until they have demonstrated their ability to capture the growing markets in the border cities, without the protection of outright embargoes and high tariffs, it seems unlikely that

Mexican producers of manufactured goods could make much of a dent in markets of the advanced countries.[148] This does not, however, exclude the possibility that Mexico could play the role of a heavy net exporter of goods in general and manufactured goods in particular, within the regional tariff walls of the Latin American Free Trade Area, or with regard to its nearby Central American neighbors. In fact, both the phenomena just mentioned have already come to pass on a modest but growing scale. Table 37 shows Mexico's recent trade balances with its sister republics in Latin America. Over half of the exports shipped to them have been made up of manufactured goods in recent years. And, finally, Mexican industrial capitalists have also shown a remarkable measure of economic aggressiveness in expanding their operations to the south, via direct private foreign investments in neighboring countries.

Table 37

Mexico's Trade Balances with Latin American Nations, 1961-63
(Millions of current pesos)

Trade Balance	With CACM[a]	With LAFTA[b]	With All Latin America
1961 Balance	+ 96.9	+ 46.8	+ 206.3
Exports	101.1	98.5	398.2
Imports	4.2	51.7	191.9
1962 Balance	+ 114.1	+ 132.4	+ 278.2
Exports	117.2	208.8	505.8
Imports	3.1	76.0	227.6
1963 Balance	+ 126.4	+ 189.3	+ 392.6
Exports	139.0	324.8	690.0
Imports	12.6	135.5	297.4

Notes: [a]Central American Common Market members.

[b]Latin American Free Trade Area.

Sources: Comercio Exterior, monthly English edition, March, 1964, pp. 2, 17; July, 1965, pp. 18-21.

The subtle irony inherent in this sort of development has not been lost on Mexico's neighbors:

> Not too long ago, at an inter-American conference, a delegate from Central America suddenly launched into what promised to be a prolonged tirade against the iniquities of 'the colossus of the North.' At that, the Mexican delegate, whose countrymen are fond of making such speeches themselves, settled back for a comfortable doze. His slumbers, however, came to an abrupt end when it dawned upon him that this particular blast was being leveled not at the U.S. but at Mexico.
>
> . . . .
>
> Central Americans have been unsettled by the growing tendency of Mexican businessmen to move south with an aggressiveness similar to that displayed by Yanqui capitalists in Mexico. According to one Mexico City editor, 'Mexico is behaving like a young man who has just noticed that the freckle-faced girl next door is growing up.' But the analogy that leaps to Central American lips is a different one: 'the new octopus.'[149]

Notes to Chapter 4

1. See the notes to Table 22.

2. See Report of the Combined Mexican Working Party, The Economic Development of Mexico (Baltimore: Johns Hopkins Press, 1953), pp. 348-51.

3. See the annual Balance of Payments statements in the Banco de México's Informe(s) Anual(es), parts of which are given in Table 43.

4. Specifically, for the period 1946-58, Coppock found variations about the trend in Mexico's export earnings to be less unstable than those experienced by seventy other countries in a sample of eighty-three. See Joseph D. Coppock, International Economic Instability (New York: McGraw-Hill Book Company, 1962), p. 50.

5. For a detailed disaggregation of changes in earnings on the current account of the balance of payments, see Table 43 in the Statistical Appendix.

6. For details, see Figure 1 and Table 42.

7. Unfortunately, during the late 1950's, the prices of almost all of Mexico's important exports declined at once.

8. The chart does not show the temporary war-induced surge of textile export earnings. This performance was an ephemeral one, based on an abnormally favorable demand side situation. For a discussion of it, see the Report of the Combined Mexican Working Party, *op. cit.*, pp. 67-70.

9. Except for the fact that petroleum temporarily became the number one export industry during the 1920's.

10. This contradicts "trade-gap" expectations of services deficits for most developing countries. (See Chapter 1.)

11. Dirección General de Estadística, *Anuario Estadístico, 1960-61* (Mexico: Talleres Gráficos Nacionales, 1963), p. 106.

12. In recent years, crude estimates of the number of border crossings put the figure "in the neighborhood of 100 million per year." See U.S. Department of Commerce, *Report of the Review Committee for Balance of Payments Statistics* (Washington, D.C.: U.S. Government Printing Office, 1965), p. 37.

13. *Anuario Estadístico, 1960-61*, *op. cit.*, p. 109.

14. *Ibid.*

15. The methods of estimating both tourist and border visitor expenditures are briefly discussed in Appendix A.

16. This, at any rate, is the finding of Etienne H. Miller, a U.S. Commerce Department economist. See his article (in the *Survey of Current Business*) cited in Table 24, shown below. It confirms findings of the Combined Mexican Working Party (*op. cit.*, p. 378), covering the 1940's, with specific reference to Mexico.

17. The Canadians, incidentally, are the second most important group of tourists who visit Mexico.

18. The rapid expansion of the U.S. interstate highway system has undoubtedly brought Mexico closer, in an economic sense, to much of the United States.

Aside from the transportation costs, it is extremely difficult to compare the prices of other items in the tourist's budget on an international basis. An imperfect indication of the magnitudes involved might be gleaned, however, from data comparing the cost of living for U.N. personnel in various major cities of the world. For 1965, the cost of living in Mexico City was reported as 93 vis-à-vis the 100 (New York City) base of the U.N. index. This was almost exactly equal to the mean score of 92 for the entire 54 city sample, and was within 10 per cent of the scores cited for Montreal, Geneva, Athens, Copenhagen, Paris, and Washington, D.C. Moreover, Mexico City is generally assumed to be the most expensive major city to live in (or visit) within Mexico. From the viewpoint of U.S. travelers from the rapidly growing southwestern United States, a visit to Mexico undoubtedly appears less expensive than a "comparable" visit to a Canadian or European city, or even a visit to New York or other distant parts of the U.S.

The U.N. international cost-of-living data mentioned above were taken from: U.N. Statistical Office, Retail Price Comparisons for International Salary Determination, Statistical Papers Series M-14, add. 3 (New York: United Nations, 1966), pp. 1-10.

19. See Table 3.

20. NAFIN, Nacional Financiera en el Desarrollo Económico de México, 1934-64 (México, D.F.: NAFIN, 1965), p. 23.

21. And excellent connections by road, rail, and air to Acapulco are also available at Mexico City.

22. For example, according to the Foreign Trade Bank (Banco Nacional de Comercio Exterior), 25,000 new hotel and motel rooms were added to the nation's tourist accommodations between 1953 and 1961. See Mexico, 1963

(Yearbook), p. 242.

23. On this point, see any of the series of border city studies published by PRONAF (Programa Nacional Fronteriza), e.g., Nuevo Laredo (México, D.F.: Talleres Gráficos Nacionales, 1961).

24. Such as Acapulco and Taxco in the otherwise very poor state of Guerrero, and Cuernavaca in the relatively underdeveloped state of Morelos.

25. See Report of the Combined Mexican Working Party, op. cit., pp. 348, 360.

26. Also, as with other cotton selling nations, Mexico had to contend with the rapid growth of synthetic fibers.

27. It is interesting to note that, in volume terms, the world's cotton trade apparently did not collapse during the Great Depression.

28. See Table 46 for a series of wholesale prices paid for Mexican cotton for the period 1939-63.

29. FAO, Commodity Review, 1964, Special Supplement (Rome: FAO, 1965), p. II-79.

30. FAO, Commodity Review, 1965 (Rome: FAO, 1965), p. 143.

31. India, in fact, has lately become a net importer of cotton. Pakistan normally imports only miniscule amounts of cotton, but the volume of its exports has fallen sharply since the early 1950's. (See Table 26 and the sources cited therein.)

32. In fact, as of 1950, even the normally huge surpluses held by the U.S. Commodity Credit Corporation temporarily disappeared as the world price of cotton rose well above the U.S. domestic support price.

33. The recent westward shift in the center of gravity of U.S. cotton growing has also been based on a move to irrigated land. See James H. Street, The New Revolution in the Cotton Economy (Chapel Hill: University of North Carolina Press, 1957).

34. See Table 50. Also, much of the rest of the cotton crop was undoubtedly grown on land serviced by private irrigation works, mainly artesian wells. See U.S. Department of Agriculture, Foreign Agricultural Report No. 98, Mexican Cotton (Washington, D.C.: U.S. Government Printing Office, 1958), p. 18.

35. See Tables 48 and 49.

36. See USDA, Mexican Cotton, op. cit., pp. 21-23, and Comercio Exterior, monthly, English ed., September, 1964, p. 16.

37. The roads connecting the northern states with U.S. cities are especially important in this regard, since most of the exported cotton is transshipped through the United States. Ibid., p. 17.

38. Specifically, the so-called Compensatory Exchange program requires would-be importers of commodities that must have import licenses to show evidence of having arranged for the export of an equivalent value of cotton. This compels foreigners who want to sell in Mexico to help search for markets for Mexican cotton. The Mexicans have not had any abnormal carry-over of cotton.

39. See Cesar Sepulveda, A Statement of the Laws of Mexico (Washington, D.C.: Pan American Union, 1961) p. 149.

40. See USDA, Mexican Cotton, op. cit., p. 25.

41. See Table 26 for production data. Aside from the aforementioned factors, the government also acts to encourage cotton production in another important way, i.e., it actively encourages research aimed at producing new and better seeds, farming techniques, etc. On the foregoing points, see USDA, Mexican Cotton, op. cit., pp. 36-38; and USDA, Foreign Agricultural Service Report No. 99, Mexico as a Market and Competitor for U.S. Agriculture Products, op. cit., (Washington, D.C.: U.S. Government Printing Office, 1958), p. 14.

42. For a discussion of these programs, see USDA, Economic Research Service Report No. 77, Termination of

the Bracero Program (Washington, D.C.: U.S. Government Printing Office, 1965).

43. Harland Padfield and William E. Martin, Farmers, Workers, and Machines (Tucson: The University of Arizona Press, 1965), pp. 276-80; pp. 193-217.

44. Ellen C. Garwood, Will Clayton (Austin: University of Texas Press, 1958), p. 102.

45. James H. Budd, "The Anderson-Clayton Story," Mexican-American Review, September, 1963, pp. 21-27.

46. USDA, Mexican Cotton, op. cit., p. 16.

47. Ibid. Also, for a thorough analysis of the nature and extent of mechanization of cotton farming operations in northern Mexico, as of the mid-1950's, see Luis Yáñez Pérez, Mecanización de la Agricultura Mexicana (México, D.F.: Instituto Méxicano de Investigaciones Económicas, 1957), especially p. 124.

48. The $3 billion figure, of course, does not fully reflect exchange savings (from the side of imports) due to the maintenance of self-sufficiency in the face of the rapid rise in home consumption shown in Table 26.

49. On this point, see Banco Nacional de México, S.A., Review of the Economic Situation of Mexico, May, 1959, p. 9, where it is alleged that the real wages of ejidatarios in northern Mexico expanded sixfold (or more) between 1930 and 1958. Ejidatarios are members of ejidos, a type of collective farm. Though ejidal land is always communally owned, it is frequently fractionated into plots which are worked individually by particular peasant households.

50. In 1964 and 1965, respectively, wheat exports brought in an estimated $36 and $41 million. See Banco de México, Informe Anual, 1965, preliminary ed., p. 60.

51. See Tables 49 and 50.

52. Report of the Combined Mexican Working Party, op. cit., p. 360.

53. The price of Santos No. 4 in New York, for example, averaged about $.09 per pound over this period compared to an average price of about $.19 per pound during the 1920's.

Mexican coffees are mild "arabica" types commanding a premium price vis-à-vis most African "robustas" and ordinary "Brazils."

54. The European market accounted for about 40 per cent of world coffee consumption before the war began. For a detailed analysis of this and other historical aspects of the development of the world coffee economy, see J.W.F. Rowe, The World's Coffee (London: Her Majesty's Stationery Office, 1963), pp, 11-20, and FAO, Commodity Bulletin Series No. 33, The World Coffee Economy (Rome: FAO, 1961), pp. 5-8. The discussion above is based on the analyses presented in the two sources just mentioned.

55. Brazil burned about 70 million bags of coffee during the 1930's. It emerged from World War II with an inventory of about 6 million bags which was completely exhausted by 1949. See Rowe, op. cit., p. 14.

56. Planted as seedlings, coffee trees begin to bear in two to four years with yields reaching their peak levels in seven to ten years.

57. For an up-to-date detailed description of the International Coffee Agreement (ICA), see Pan American Coffee Bureau, Annual Coffee Statistics, 1964 (New York: Pan American Coffee Bureau, 1965), pp. 1-14. See Rowe, op. cit., pp. 15-19, 186-91, for a discussion of earlier agreements.

58. The single most significant exception is Indonesia, which has yet to approximate its prewar production levels, or its earlier export performances.

59. Rowe, op. cit., p. 31.

60. Besides experiencing a decline in its share of world coffee exports, Brazil's share of world production has also fallen sharply, from about two-thirds during the early 1930's to about one-half as of the early 1960's. See FAO, The World Coffee Economy, op. cit., p. 47.

61. Rowe, op. cit., p. 24. Since coffee consumption would probably not respond very rapidly to price declines, the results of such a move by Brazil would be disastrous--as it was the last time they tried aggressive price competition--during the late 1930's.

62. Rowe, op. cit., p. 30.

63. See Table 41.

64. As of 1961, Chiapas, Guerrero, and Oaxaca (three of the poorest states in Mexico), accounted for about half of the coffee harvest. See Anuario Estadístico, 1962-63, op. cit., p. 326. Yates, op. cit., pp. 79-83, shows that these states received a very small share of the direct benefits of public investment programs.

65. See Comercio Exterior, monthly English edition, April, 1962, p. 15.

66. Ibid., August, 1964, p. 10.

67. FAO, The World Coffee Economy, op. cit., p. 10.

68. Report of the Combined Mexican Working Party, op. cit., pp. 158-59.

69. Sugar has been cultivated and refined in Mexico for about 400 years. During the first three decades of this century, it occasionally appeared on the export list. On a net basis, however, sugar was typically imported for many years prior to the Korean War. Compare Tables 6 and 7, pp. 44-69 in FAO, The World Sugar Economy in Figures, 1880-1959, Commodity Reference Series No. 1 (Rome: FAO, 1960).

70. See Figure 1, above, and Table 42.

71. The historical data on the area planted to cane are spotty. However, it appears that it expanded by about 250 per cent between 1939 and 1960, from about 120 to 315 thousand hectares. See Anuario Estadístico, 1940, op. cit., p. 508, and Anuario Estadístico, 1961-62, op. cit., pp. 350-64.

72. See Table 50. Also, as of 1960, almost 20 per cent of the crop, by value, was grown in the northern states of

Sinaloa and Tamaulipas, according to data reported in Anuario Estadístico, 1962-63, op. cit., pp. 326-327.

73. On this point, see, for example, Thomas T. Poleman, The Papaloapan Project (Palo Alto, California: Stanford University Press, 1964), p. 125.

74. As of 1961, three-eighths of the sugar crop, by value, was still grown in Vera Cruz. See Anuario Estadístico, 1962-63, op. cit., pp. 326-327.

75. On this point, see, for example, "Mexico and the International Sugar Trade," Comercio Exterior, monthly English edition, December, 1958, pp. 4-5, and May, 1962, pp. 9-10.

76. The quota system is an integral part of the U.S. government's subsidization program for the domestic beet and cane sugar growers. By restricting supplies available in the U.S. market, the price of sugar there (even net of import duties) has generally been held above world market prices, leading to intensive competition for shares of the U.S. quota. For recent data on the price spread, see FAO, Commodity Review, 1965 (Rome: FAO, 1965), p. 83.

77. Quotas under the British Commonwealth Sugar Agreement are published, along with U.S. quotas, in the various issues of International Sugar Council, Sugar Yearbook (e.g., 1964, pp. 318-20.

78. France has special importing arrangements worked out with its overseas dependencies, such as Madagascar. See FAO, Commodity Review, 1965, p. 88.

79. For the period 1959-61, the last three years the ISA was in effect, roughly half the total value of sugar traded in world commerce moved under the agreement--with most of the remainder moving under the other "special arrangements" as mentioned above--at prices typically higher than the "world market price." On the latter points, see FAO, Commodity Review, 1964, Special Supplement, Rome: FAO, 1965), p. II-44.

80. See, for example, Comercio Exterior, monthly English edition, December, 1958, p. 4.

81. See Table 29.

82. Since 1960, much of Cuba's sugar has been diverted to Communist Bloc countries. Aside from opening "Cuba's share" of the U.S. market to other non-Communist countries, this had the temporary effect of generally reducing supply side pressures in the world sugar market, leading to a rapid rise in the "world market price" of sugar during 1962 and 1963.

83. See Table 29.

84. For a somewhat dated but still relevant analysis of Mexico's export effort along these lines, see USDA, Foreign Agricultural Report No. 99, Mexico as a Market and Competitor for U.S. Agricultural Products (Washington, D.C.: U.S. Government Printing Office, 1957), especially pp. 36-43. This report also discusses various other minor Mexican agricultural exports, e.g., pineapples, bananas, peanuts, which will not be treated here.

85. Thus, it is estimated that $36 and $42 million worth of wheat were exported in 1964 and 1965, respectively, while $16 and $77 million worth of corn were also sold abroad. See Banco de México, Informe Anual, 1965, preliminary ed., p. 61.

86. See Table 42.

87. Report of the Combined Mexican Working Party, op. cit., p. 360.

88. FAO, Livestock in Latin America (New York: United Nations, 1962), p. 39.

89. Ibid., pp. 40-42.

90. For example, the export quota for 1966 has been sharply reduced from that of 1965 in order to assure an increased flow of cattle toward the Federal District where acute shortages have been reported. See Banco Nacional de México, Review of the Economic Situation in Mexico, December, 1965, pp. 7-9.

91. For a discussion of this point, see USDA, Foreign Agriculture, January 6, 1964, p. 11.

92. Ibid., December 30, 1963, p. 8.

93. See Comercio Exterior, monthly English edition, June, 1961, p. 21.

94. Assuming, of course, that the U.S. Government does not use its beef import quotas to limit Mexico's shipments to that country.

95. Report of the Combined Mexican Working Party, op. cit., p. 390.

96. See Table 42.

97. U.S. Department of the Interior, Commercial Fisheries Review, November, 1964, p. 99. Abalone, lobster, and tuna account for virtually all the rest of these export earnings.

98. As of 1963, 99 per cent.

99. Specifically, U.S. shrimp consumption per capita rose from .48 pounds in 1939 to .78 pounds in 1950, 1.03 pounds in 1955, and 1.18 pounds in 1960. For further details concerning consumption trends, see U.S. Tariff Commission, Report on Investigation No. 332-40: Shrimp (Washington, D.C.: U.S. Government Printing Office, March, 1961), p. 64. (Hereinafter called the Shrimp Report.) See also Column (4) of Table 30, p. 89, which may be taken as a rough measure of aggregate shrimp consumption in the U.S.

100. For a discussion of this point, see pp. 41-52, 64-69 of the Shrimp Report. Also see pp. 79-81 describing the transportation channels used for distributing shrimp in the United States, where it is shown that it is most economical to ship shrimp in frozen form, usually by truck.

101. For example, see Quick Frozen Foods, April, 1953, pp. 5-7.

102. U.S. packers were instrumental in providing credit and technical assistance to speed up the expansion of Mexican shrimping operations. On this, see Mexican-American Review, November, 1950, pp. 10-34.

103. Ibid.

104. Ibid., and Commercial Fisheries Review, op. cit., November, 1964, pp. 100-102.

105. Ibid. By 1963, these two states accounted for 44 of the national total catch of 73 thousand metric tons.

106. According to the Shrimp Report, op. cit., p. 149, Panama, El Salvador, and Ecuador had become the most significant secondary foreign sources of shrimp by 1960.

107. On this point, see Mexican-American Review, August, 1958, pp. 20-21.

108. See Quick Frozen Foods, November, 1956.

109. Shrimp Report, op. cit., pp. 125-26.

110. In general, the largest integrated mining companies, which were mostly foreign-owned until the recent drive to "Mexicanize" the industry, work ore bodies which contain viable concentrations of copper, lead, zinc, and silver and gold. For a detailed technical discussion of this point, see U.S. Department of the Interior, Minerals Yearbook, 1964, Vol. IV (Washington, D.C.: U.S. Government Printing Office, 1965), pp. 971-74.

111. For a brief discussion of the subject, see Bela Balassa, Trade Prospects for Developing Countries (Homewood, Ill.: Richard D. Irwin, 1964), pp. 301-6, 313-20 and the annual editions of GATT, International Trade, (Geneva, GATT), sections on mineral exports.

112. Thus, during the 1950's, for example, the total value of copper, lead, and zinc traded reached cyclical peaks in 1952 and 1956, with sharp subsequent recessions. See Coppock, op. cit., p. 43 and the GATT studies just cited.

113. See Coppock, op. cit., p. 46.

114. On this point, see U.S. Department of the Interior, Mineral Facts and Problems, 1965 (Washington, D.C.: U.S. Government Printing Office, 1965), pp. 505-1, 100.

115. American Bureau of Metals Statistics, 1960 Yearbook (New York: The Maple Press Co., 1961), p. 139.

116. Mineral Facts and Problems, 1965, op. cit., pp. 290, 505, 1,100.

117. For a detailed technical discussion of the depletion problem in the various mining industries in Mexico, see Banco de México, Departamento de Investigaciones Industriales, Riqueza Minera y Yacamientos Minerales de México, presented at the XXth Session of the International Geological Conference (México, D.F.: Talleres Gráficos Nacionales, 1956). Also see Report of the Combined Mexican Working Party, op. cit., pp. 39-42.

118. See Harvard Law School, International Program in Taxation, Taxation in Mexico (Boston: Little, Brown and Co., 1957), pp. 355-63, for a description of the mineral production and export taxes levied by the Mexican Government.

119. United Nations, World Economic Survey, 1963, Vol. I (New York: United Nations, 1964), pp. 111. Also, for specific U.S. duties, see American Bureau of Metal Statistics, 1964 Yearbook, op. cit., p. 144.

120. The Report of the Combined Mexican Working Party, op. cit., pp. 42-44, indicates there was a paucity of investment in the mining sector in the 1940's because of low profit, high taxes, etc.

121. On February 6, 1961, the nation's basic mining law was substantially revised. Extant mining concessions held by foreign-controlled companies were confirmed as valid for at least another twenty-five years. But only Mexican-controlled companies were made eligible for new concessions. Also, a 50 per cent reduction in the mining production and export duties was offered to any foreign-controlled company that sold out its majority interest to indigenous elements. Since 1961, many of the most important foreign mining companies have responded to these incentives and pressures by selling out. For example, in August of 1963, Compania Minera Frisco (the world's fifth largest producer of zinc and fourteenth ranking lead producer) sold out its majority interest to the government's foreign trade bank. The company had been

controlled by British and U.S. investors. Dozens of other major foreign-owned companies have since followed suit. For a running account of the process, see the various monthly (English) editions of Comercio Exterior, especially July, 1964, pp. 10-11, and August, 1964, pp. 7-8.

122. This analysis follows the discussion presented in Mineral Facts and Problems, 1965, op. cit., p. 817.

123. See Mineral Facts and Problems, 1965, op. cit., p. 813.

124. Ibid., p. 394.

125. For an outline of the program, see Comercio Exterior, monthly Spanish edition, June, 1965, p. 415.

126. The Tehuantepec ore body is being exploited via the Frasch process.

127. Paul Ambrose, "Sulfur and Pyrites," U.S. Department of the Interior, Mineral Facts and Problems, 1965, op. cit., pp. 901-18. The remainder of this discussion generally follows Ambrose's findings.

128. To assure the future supply for domestic consumption, the government has limited exports in any one year to 10 per cent of proven reserves in the same year. This policy, it is hoped, will force the two large foreign-owned companies, which produce almost all the sulfur, to seek out new ore bodies. See Comercio Exterior, monthly Spanish edition, May, 1965, pp. 349-50.

129. Ambrose, op. cit., p. 918.

130. Report of the Combined Mexican Working Party, op. cit., p. 125.

131. The U.S. petroleum import quota, for example, was not applied to Mexico or Canada, and the United States is Mexico's only important outlet for oil and gas. See Comercio Exterior, monthly English edition, June, 1959, p. 9.

132. Ibid., April, 1958, pp. 2-4.

133. World Petroleum Report, March 15, 1965, p. 50.

134. Secretaría de Industria y Comercio, Compendio Estadístico, 1962 (México: Talleres Gráficos Nacionales, 1963), p. 116.

135. Their combined importance in this respect has fallen somewhat in recent years, as shown in Figure 1.

136. That is, tomatoes, melons, peanuts, manganese, fluorspar, barium sulfate, etc.

137. In 1964, for example, another 5 per cent of merchandise export earnings was due to the $52 million worth of wheat and maize exported, in comparison with less than $5 million thus earned in 1963 and an estimated $119 million for 1965.

138. Even a few years ago, this was not the case in that much of the cotton grown in the Matamoros district went straight from the fields to gins on the U.S. side of the border, there to be cleaned, packed, and transhipped elsewhere.

139. For example, for 1963 and 1964 combined, $9 million worth of henequen fiber was exported versus $50 million worth of henequen manufactures. See Banco de México, Informe Anual, 1964, pp. 88-89.

140. For 1963 and 1964 combined, $49 million worth of meat exports were in the form of processed carcasses versus $60 million worth of beef on-the-hoof. Ibid.

141. Yates, op. cit., pp. 210-19.

142. Ibid.

For a detailed breakdown of exports, by value, by customs exit, see Anuario Estadístico, 1962-63, op. cit., p. 516.

143. The following data from U.N., Yearbook of International Trade Statistics, 1963 (New York: United Nations, 1965), pp. 479-81 (millions of pesos) provide the basis for the ensuing discussion:

Value of Mexico's Exports by SITC Group Numbers, 1960-63

	500's	600's (net of 680's)	700's	800's	Total Value
1960	226	605	109	179	9,540
1961	335	765	123	173	10,311
1962	400	771	112	183	11,614
1963	445	1,083	135	234	12,300

144. The single most important item in the latter group being exports of "books and other printed matter" worth about $8 million in 1963.

145. Including, of course, the minor mineral and agricultural exports only briefly mentioned.

146. During World War II, textiles temporarily played a major export role, but only because of the very favorable and abnormal conditions in the U.S. market at the time.

147. That is, by granting special fiscal concessions to encourage the export of highly fabricated goods. See Comercio Exterior, monthly English edition, November, 1961, pp. 1,4.

148. Mexico is not a contracting party to the GATT. It frequently completely closes down imports of manufactured goods to protect home producers.

149. Newsweek, January 10, 1966, p. 38.

CHAPTER 5 SUMMARY OF FINDINGS

MEXICO'S GROWTH AND THE "TRADE-GAP" DILEMMA

Over the past quarter of a century, external economic difficulties have not prevented Mexico from achieving a sustained and rapid rate of economic growth. The foregoing analyses of the various aspects of Mexico's adaptation to its external economic environment allow an interpretation of the entire process in terms of the "trade-gap" line of reasoning. Since the target growth rates posited in such studies have, in fact, been matched or exceeded, it is evident that enough foreign exchange has become available to finance Mexico's "irreducible import needs." The relevant question is: How?

One possible explanation turns on the issue of capital inflows. "Trade-gap" studies make explicit attempts to estimate the volume of capital that would have to be transferred toward the poor countries (as a group) to enable them to avoid an import bottleneck in pursuing their growth aspirations under existing conditions in world commerce. The necessary transfer is simply the difference between their estimated "irreducible import needs" consistent with target growth achievement, and the estimated magnitude of their total exchange earnings. The United Nations alleges that about two-fifths of the import needs of the poor countries would have to be supplied in this manner, if they were (as a group) to achieve growth rates such as those experienced in Mexico since 1940. More conservative estimates (for example, Balassa's) put it as low as two-sevenths of import requirements. On this count, it should first be noted that Mexico's experience during the 1940's was essentially an internally financed operation, as shown in Table 14. Since then, the portion of imports financed via a net inflow of capital has clearly risen. But it has not yet begun to take on the dimensions suggested by Balassa or the U.N.

Parenthetically, it is interesting to note that the growing

inflow of capital and a gradual shift toward a less expansionary domestic monetary policy has enabled the Mexican Government to reduce inflationary pressures in the economy. Relative domestic price stability, by Latin American standards, has been achieved over the past few years without resort to a substantial increase in the over-all tax burden and without paying a high price in terms of growth achievement.

Mexico's proven ability to service the "import needs" consistent with rapid growth achievement, then, has not been based simply on gaining access to enough foreign capital to cover a current account deficit of the magnitude envisioned in the "trade-gap" studies. Rather, the current account deficit itself has been held within more modest and manageable limits than those envisioned in such studies, with capital inflows filling a relatively small gap. This, in turn, has been accomplished via a steady expansion of exchange earnings and a check on the rapid growth of the nation's "irreducible import needs" via import substitution. Fortunately, it was not necessary for Mexico to mount its export drive in the face of a secular deterioration in its commodity terms of trade. Rather, it seems that the terms of trade improved a bit, on the average, between 1940 and the mid-1960's.

After making allowances for the secular rise in import prices, it appears that the Mexicans have managed, roughly speaking, to bring about a fourfold expansion in their "earned capacity to import," since 1940. The single most important source of expansion in the export base of the economy has been the growth of the tourist industry and the border trade. In expanding their earnings on the latter account, the Mexicans have clearly capitalized on their locational advantage with respect to the rapidly growing U.S. travel market. This source of earnings cannot, however, be regarded simply as a windfall. The nation's political and economic infrastructure had to be intensively developed to seriously earn that sorely needed exchange.

Aside from the spectacular growth of travel account earnings, very respectable gains have also been registered on account of various merchandise exports, almost without exception in world markets for primary products. Some of the gains were made at the expense of other developing countries. For example, along with the African producers, Mexico expanded its share of the world coffee market mainly at the expense of Brazil. Moreover, Mexico's ability to sell a much larger bundle of sugar to the United States has clearly been made possible by Cuba's withdrawal from that market.

But the Mexicans have also competed quite successfully with the advanced countries in certain other cases. The rapid expansion of Mexico's shrimp exports resulted from a decisive move into the once self-sufficient U.S. market. Even in the case of cotton, the most important commodity export, it is clear that a part of Mexico's impressive gain there has been at the expense of the United States, though other developing countries (mainly India and Pakistan) have also experienced losses in the postwar reallocation of that market.

Only the traditional metal mining industries turned in distinctly poor export performances. There can be no doubt that Mexico's export effort was seriously impaired by U.S. lead and zinc policies. Nonetheless, it is also obvious that the domestic metal mining industry has serious supply problems of an economic and institutional nature. It is the only case where there is abundant evidence to support an argument to the effect that government policy toward an industry has on balance retarded its export performance.

Turning to the question of the evolution of Mexico's "irreducible import needs," it is interesting to note that Mexico's imports apparently have not, on the average, grown more rapidly than aggregate output. Although the import coefficient rose during the immediate postwar period, it has since then fallen to prewar levels. Even so, the absolute volume of imports has risen quite rapidly, and major secular changes in the composition of the economy's "import needs" have been witnessed. For example, a rapid expansion of light manufacturing industries, under an umbrella of commercial policy protection, has apparently greatly reduced the "need" for imports of many types of consumer goods. The phenomenal expansion of the iron and steel and cement industries has brought about a decline in the need for imported construction materials. The significant progress achieved in the agricultural sector of the economy has also had a profound effect on the composition of the country's "irreducible import needs." At the outset of the period of rapid growth, certain basic food items, such as sugar, wheat, and corn, were being imported; but self-sufficiency, and even a modest export capability, has now been achieved with respect to each of them.

All told, therefore, an ongoing and pervasive process of import substitution has clearly helped to keep Mexico's growth efforts from coming to grief on the horns of the "trade-gap" dilemma. By checking the growth of Mexico's "irreducible import needs," it has served to keep pressures on the balance of payments within tolerable limits, that is, within the country's capacity to earn foreign exchange and attract foreign capital.

THE RELEVANCE OF MEXICO'S EXPERIENCE FOR OTHER DEVELOPING COUNTRIES

Very few of the other developing countries have enjoyed rates of growth comparable to Mexico's since 1940, and many of them still face serious external economic difficulties. Unfortunately, it is not possible to report that the Mexicans have found any sort of new, easy formula for dealing with the hard problems posed in "trade-gap" studies. They have not found a way to help their rapidly growing manufacturing industries break into new export markets on any appreciable scale. In fact, much of their small export bundle of manufactured goods was shown to be destined for other poor countries.

Moreover, a part of their export expansion has basically involved a more systematic exploitation of their natural locational advantage. A fortuitous discovery of one of the world's major sulfur deposits helped to expand exchange earnings. Also, cases have been cited in which Mexico's export gains have been directly tied to corresponding losses for other poor countries.

Nonetheless, it is quite apparent that the Mexicans have demonstrated the trade advantages that can be gleaned from a policy of active promotion of the agricultural sector of the economy. Their efforts in this respect, as noted above, have had payoffs on both sides of the trade ledger. Practically all their basic food items, and most other agricultural products that they can produce economically, are off the import list. Many developing countries, perhaps mistakenly, tend to count such items among their "irreducible import needs." Also, in a number of significant cases, the merchandise exports in which the Mexicans have experienced major gains have been agricultural exports. When U.S. policy in the world cotton market permitted it, the Mexicans were among the few developing countries in a position to take advantage of an opportunity to penetrate that market. When the break came in the world sugar market, the Mexicans again were ready to move, from the side of supply.

Finally, although the border trade with the United States is clearly a phenomenon based on location, that is less true of the tourist industry. Chapter 4 showed that almost half of the tourists now enter Mexico by plane, and cited Mexico City as their principal destination. Numerous other Latin American capital cities are within a comparable economic radius of major U.S. urban centers. Here, at least, is one major example of a truly dynamic market in the advanced countries that is wide open to the developing countries if they are willing, and make themselves able, to exploit it. The Mexicans have been willing to cater to tourists and have made their country hospitable to outsiders, earning over a billion dollars in foreign exchange in the process since World War II. Greece also thrives on U.S. (and European) tourists. It is a long way from Chicago, or even New York, and it is, too, an underdeveloped country.

EXPORT EXPANSION, IMPORT SUBSTITUTION, AND THE INCOME DISTRIBUTION PROBLEM IN MEXICO

Although the rapid expansion of the export sector of the economy has clearly played a vital role in promoting Mexico's over-all growth achievements, it must also be recognized that it has helped to foster and perpetuate the nation's rather serious income distribution problem. The profound skew in the national size distribution of family incomes is strongly conditioned by very wide interregional differences in mean family incomes, on the order of six to one, between the richest and the poorest states. (See Chapter 2.) Moreover, aside from the Federal District, the far northern states are easily the richest in the country, with Northern Baja California actually enjoying a higher average income level than the Federal District.

Throughout the discussion of the export sector of the economy in Chapter 4, attention was focused on the regional incidence of the major export industries. Drawing the findings there together leaves very little doubt about the over-all regional bias of the expansion that has lately occurred in the export base of the economy. The border trade is the largest and most rapidly expanding source of foreign exchange. The very definition of it defines its regional impact. Data concerning the bona fide tourists (presented in Chapter 4) indicate that they heavily favor the Federal District as the place in Mexico to visit. This only reinforces the traditionally pre-eminent position of that region.

In merchandise exports, cotton was found to be by far the most important primary product exported. As of 1960, 96 per cent of it (by value) was grown in the eight far northern states. The center of the shrimping industry was also found to be in the far north, as are many of the major nonferrous metal mining districts. Even the petroleum industry is heavily concentrated in Tamaulipas, the northernmost Gulf state. Of the major commodity exports, only coffee, sulfur, and sugar clearly make substantial direct contributions to the economic well-being of areas outside the Federal District and the rich northern states. Furthermore, most of the value added to commodity exports, via processing, occurs in plants that are heavily concentrated in the far north.

Yates has argued that the extreme concentration of manufacturing activities in the immediate vicinity of the Federal District not only unnecessarily promotes an undue concentration of wealth there, but may actually be anti-economic. He suggests a series of fiscal and other reforms that would reverse the present government policies now serving only to encourage a polarization of industrial expansion around the Federal District.

But the regional concentration of the major export industries presents a different sort of problem. Although it is possible to attempt to influence the location of new factories, how can one move the northern border, or the location of the mines in Chihuahua and Sonora, or the shrimp in the Bay of California, or the already established cotton (and wheat) belt in the irrigation districts of the north? Or, would it impress anyone as being economically rational to move the export processing activities away from both their sources of raw materials and the border they are most likely to cross?

Finally, adding to the complexity of the problem, the most promising single opportunity to carry forward the process of import substitution apparently lies precisely in the already rich far northern border region. In the discussion of

Table 38

Monthly Consumption of Foreign Products in Tijuana and Mexicali, Baja California, 1962
(In thousands of Mexican pesos)

	Tijuana		Mexicali	
	Total Consumption	Imports	Total Consumption	Imports
Fuels and lubricants	11,551	1,451	13,294	1,720
Foods, drinks, tobacco	38,888	25,046	41,605	25,427
Footwear	2,129	1,443	2,039	1,040
Garments	6,594	3,881	4,743	2,784
Chemicals and pharmaceuticals	5,348	1,805	14,780	6,311
Wood and wooden furniture	3,415	1,025	2,620	786
Paper and paper products	1,400	1,162	1,054	874
Magazines and books	1,686	303	1,064	191
Non-metallic mineral products	3,455	1,590	3,622	1,450
Machinery and equipment; household appliances	4,937	3,580	6,424	4,184
Transportation equipment	6,971	6,968	7,320	7,316
Other manufactures	3,837	2,492	2,873	1,862
Textiles	247	124	495	156
Metallic products	3,455	1,590	3,623	1,450
Total	94,611	52,460	105,556	55,551

Source: Banco de México, Departamento de Estudios Económicos Regionales, as reported in *Review of the Economic Situation of Mexico*, April, 1964, p. 8.

the import aspects of the border trade (roughly a quarter billion dollar debit item in the current account of the balance of payments), it was noted that exchange outlays on this account are thought to consist mainly of unrecorded imports of consumer goods into the border region. Although comprehensive data substantiating the exact nature of this trade are unfortunately not available, some scattered clues can be gleaned from occasional surveys made by various official government agencies. Table 38 summarizes the findings of a recent study concerning the nature and over-all importance of imports into two of the largest border cities, rich cities in the terms of per family incomes, and among the fastest growing in terms of population.

The significance of this phenomenon has apparently been missed by some economists (for example, Raymond Vernon) who have lately studied the Mexican economy and found that the relatively straightforward steps in the process of import substitution have nearly been exhausted and that, "For the present, therefore, import replacement may be slowed down by problems of scale and by technical bottlenecks."[1] The major items on the "import list" in Table 38 are all already produced in Mexico. If they are unable to compete in these dynamic markets along their own border (but outside the tariff umbrella), Mexican producers of such manufactured goods can hardly be judged ready to break into foreign markets, even if commercial barriers to entry there should be dropped.

But a move into the border regions, in an effort to capitalize on the opportunities for import savings there, would only further intensify the regional disparities in income levels. It is tempting to ask why the problem of regional income disparities could not simply be solved by moving the people in the underdeveloped hinterland to the border regions, where the real opportunities for rapid growth seem to lie. But, as noted in the discussion of Table 19, people _are_ moving out of the hinterland and toward these "growth poles" in droves. However, there are just as many remaining behind. The population growth rate permits both things to happen at once.

Note to Chapter 5

1. Raymond Vernon, _The Dilemma of Mexico's Development_ (Cambridge: Harvard University Press, 1963), p. 183.

APPENDIX A

APPENDIX A

A NOTE ON MEXICAN DATA SOURCES

More than a decade ago, the Combined Mexican Working Party, with complete access to all the data sources within the Mexican Government agencies, had this to say about the coverage and reliability of official statistics:

> In most fields, the official statistics are incomplete or inaccurate or both, and in some instances discrepancies have proved baffling. . . . There is a real need in Mexico to improve official statistics and to integrate the activities of agencies engaged in collecting or regrouping statistics.[1]

Unfortunately, the quotation is still timely. In fact, much valuable historical data laboriously pieced together by the Working Party have not been kept up-to-date since then. To cite but one important example, the Working Party made estimates, for the 1940's, of the factoral distribution of aggregate income.[2] That series has not been continued, and no one in Mexico really knows, for example, what the profit share of the national income is. Even the estimates of expenditures on the gross product, by major categories, are still extremely crude.[3] But the most important data deficiencies from the point of view of this study are those connected with the balance of payments and trade statistics. The major problem with the current account items in the balance of payments concerns the reliability of the estimates of total earnings and payments on the travel accounts. The estimates of expenditures of bona fide tourists may not be a bad approximation of the actual outlays of that group. These bona fide tourists are accurately counted since they need to have passes to travel in the country. Also, a survey sample of their average expenditures is periodically taken with the average coverage of this sample being about one-third of the persons crossing the frontier on a given day.[4] Multiplying the head count by the average expenditure per person produces the tourism data shown in the balance of payments. The same procedure is applied to the

Mexican tourists leaving the country. It is the so-called border trade expenditure and income items that are most difficult to estimate. The problem basically lies in the fact that nobody counts the border crossings accurately, and no one systematically tries to estimate how much the border crossers spend, or exactly what they buy.[5] There are good reasons for this. It would be a monumental task, since border crossings now run upward of 100 million per year. Moreover, it might be embarrassing to both governments to find out exactly what the American border crossers buy. Hence, both the U.S. Commerce Department and the Banco de México use data on the flow of foreign currency through banks in the area, together with crude estimates of the number of border crossings, to derive their rather disparate estimates of the flow of funds at the border. The Mexicans recently revised their series downward toward the U.S. estimates, but only extrapolated the revised data backward to the mid-1950's. Hence, the discontinuity in the estimates of current account earnings shown in Table 43.

In addition, there are other problems with the current account data. The value of (nonmonetary) gold and silver exports includes a crude estimate of the value of recoverable gold and silver in exports of other metal ores. Estimates of "Bracero" remittances are crude, being based on the volume of postal and telegraphic money orders coming from the United States plus "Bracero" sales of dollars to branches of the Banco de México in border cities.

On the capital accounts, the flow of official long-term capital is, of course, accurately gauged. But estimates of capital flows on private account are subject to wide margins of error. Hence, the resulting, and occasionally rather large, errors and omissions item comes as no surprise.

It would be hazardous to regard the balance of payments data as anything more than rough estimates. The same applies to most of the other data used in the study, although the customs data concerning registered merchandise exports of particular commodities are probably reasonably accurate. The import tariff and classification schema have been revised so frequently, and the bundle of goods imported are so diverse, that it is virtually impossible for one person to work it in any meaningful way.

Notes to Appendix A

1. Report of the Combined Mexican Working Party, The Economic Development of Mexico (Baltimore: Johns Hopkins University Press, 1953), p. x.

2. Ibid., p. 171.

3. On this, see United Nations, National Accounting Practices in Sixty Countries (New York: United Nations, 1964), pp. 145-48.

4. This and the information that follows are based on a private communication to the author from the Banco de México and the source cited in the next footnote.

5. For a discussion and description of U.S. methods of estimating this phenomenon, see U.S. Department of Commerce, Report of the Review Committee for Balance of Payments Statistics (Washington, D.C.: U.S. Government Printing Office, April, 1965), pp. 37-39.

APPENDIX B

STATISTICAL TABLES

Table 39

Trends in Per Capita GNP in Real Terms, 1940-65

Year	Real GNP[a] (1)	Growth Rate[b] (2)	Population[c] (3)	GNP Per Capita[d] (4)=(1)/(3)	Growth Rate[e] (5)	GNP Deflator[f] (6)
1940	20,721	---	19.654	1,054	---	35.2
1945	31,959	---	22.514	1,420	---	64.1
1949	37,627	---	25.099	1,499	---	93.5
1950	40,577	7.8	25.791	1,573	4.9	100.0
1951	43,621	7.5	26.585	1,641	4.3	119.9
1952	45,366	4.0	27.403	1,654	.8	129.3
1953	45,618	.6	28.246	1,614	-2.4	128.1
1954	50,319	10.3	29.115	1,728	7.9	142.1
1955	54,767	8.3	30.011	1,825	5.6	160.5
1956	58,214	6.3	30.935	1,881	3.1	170.6
1957	62,708	7.9	31.887	1,967	4.6	182.1
1958	66,177	5.5	32.868	2,013	2.3	192.1
1959	68,119	2.9	33.880	2,011	- .1	199.9
1960	73,482	7.9	34.923	2,104	4.6	209.7
1961	76,038	3.5	36.091	2,107	.1	215.3
1962	79,691	4.8	37.223	2,141	1.6	222.7
1963	84,700	6.3	38.416	2,205	3.0	226.9
1964	93,200	10.0	39.643	2,350	6.6	241.0
1965	98,200	5.4	40.913	2,400	2.1	---

Notes: All data are latest revised official estimates.
--- stands for "not calculated."
[a]In millions of pesos, at 1950 market prices.
[b]Annual percentage change in (1).
[c]In millions of souls.
[d]In thousands of pesos.
[e]Annual percentage change in (4).
[f]This is the price index which, when applied to (1), generates money value of GNP for the period in question. 1950=100, the base year of the index.

Sources: Column (1), Banco de México, Informe Anual, various issues; Column (3), Nacional Financiera, 50 años de Revolución Mexicana en cifras (México: Talleres Gráficos Nacionales, 1963), p. 40; Dirección General Estadística, Anuario del Censo de Población, various issues. All other columns are derived from (1) and/or (3).

Table 40

Public Investment, Private Investment, and GNP, 1940-63
(In millions of current pesos)

Year	GNP (1)	Gross Private Investment (2)	Gross Public Investment (3)	Total Investment Coefficient $(4) = \frac{(2) + (3)}{(1)}$	Public Share of Total Investment $(5) = \frac{(3)}{(2) + (3)}$
1940	7,300	457	336	10.9	42.4
1944	17,700	1,016	724	9.8	67.4
1948	31,700	2,917	1,631	14.3	35.9
1950	40,577	3,294	2,666	14.7	44.7
1952	58,643	4,732	3,417	13.9	41.9
1954	71,540	5,400	4,365	13.6	44.7
1956	99,323	9,060	4,933	14.1	35.3
1958	127,152	10,770	6,516	13.6	37.7
1959	136,200	10,994	6,873	13.1	38.6
1960	154,137	12,000	8,772	13.5	42.2
1961	163,757	12,324	10,400	13.9	46.0
1962	177,533	12,704	11,327	13.5	47.0
1963	192,200	13,873	14,371	14.7	51.0

Note: These investment data do not include estimates of inventory accumulation.

Sources: Same as Table 39, and Nacional Financiera, *Informe Anual*, various issues.

Table 41

Selected Physical Production Data, 1940-63
(In thousands of metric tons unless otherwise specified)

Product	Year						Sources
	1940	1945	1950	1955	1960	1963	
Primary Products							
Maize	1, 640	2, 186	3, 122	4, 490	5, 386	6, 424	1, 2
Wheat	464	347	587	850	1, 190	1, 786	1, 2
Beans	97	162	250	449	528	700	1, 2
Rice	108	121	187	210	328	266	1, 2
Tomatoes	80	233	432	387	389	426	1, 2
Shrimp	4	5	18	26	40	43	1, 3
Coffee	52	55	66	93	124	138	1, 2
Iron Ore	132	353	395	429	518	1, 396	1, 2
Manganese	2	19	14	36	73	54	1, 2
Coal	816	914	911	1, 342	1, 771	2, 071	1, 2
Manufactured Goods							
Anhydrous Ammonia	---	---	8	17	20	151	1
Ammonia Sulfate	---	---	3	70	147	160	1
Simple Superphosphate	---	---	15	75	93	117	1
Caustic Soda	---	---	8	23	66	89	1

(Continued)

Table 41 (Continued)

Product	Year						Sources
	1940	1945	1950	1955	1960	1963	
Manufactured Goods (cont'd)							
Sulfuric Acid	---	---	44	125	249	390	1
Pig Iron	92	210	227	328	777	1,003	1,4
Steel Ingots	149	230	391	713	1,491	2,016	1,2
Trucks, Assembled[a]	---	---	11	20	22	26	1,2
Autos, Assembled[a]	---	---	10	13	28	50	1,2
Beer (million liters)	180	353	501	679	853	850	1,2
Sugar ('000 tons)[b]	292	373	590	901	1,426	1,638	1,2
Cigarettes (million packs)	90	1,120	1,300	1,640	1,870	1,800	1,5
Cement	485	808	1,388	2,086	3,086	3,680	1,2

Notes: [a]Thousands of units.
[b]Refined sugar.
--- stands for "not available."

Sources: (1) Nacional Financiera, Informe Anual, various issues; (2) Nacional Financiera, 50 años de Revolución Méxicana en cifras (México: Talleres Gráficos Nacionales, 1963), pp. 48-108; (3) Combined Mexican Working Party, The Economic Development of Mexico (Baltimore: Johns Hopkins Press, 1953), p. 246; (4) ECLA, Statistical Bulletin for Latin America, various issues; (5) Dirección General de Estadística, Anuario Estadístico, various issues.

Table 42

The Value and Relative Importance of Mexico's Major Merchandise Exports, 1940-64
(Value in millions of U.S. dollars)

	Year											
	1940 Value	%	1950 Value	%	1955 Value	%	1956 Value	%	1957 Value	%	1958 Value	%
Cotton[a]	--	--	139	26	252	32	263	31	173	23	190	27
Coffee	4	3	45	8	104	13	105	12	106	14	79	11
Sugar[b]	--	--	--	--	--	--	--	--	8	1	11	2
Meat[c]	3	2	--	--	18	2	8	1	20	3	54	8
Seafood	--	--	19	4	19	2	24	3	22	3	34	4
Copper[d]	9	6	25	5	67	9	73	9	37	5	30	4
Lead[e]	15	10	70	13	53	7	53	6	51	7	35	5
Zinc[f]	6	4	25	5	28	4	43	5	36	5	20	3
Sulfur	--	--	--	--	--	--	14	2	22	3	23	3
Petroleum[g]	17	12	32	6	50	6	53	6	38	5	29	4
Gold[h] and Silver	62	42	50	9	48	6	43	5	52	7	49	7
(12 products above)	116	(79)	405	(76)	639	(81)	679	(80)	565	(75)	554	(78)
All others	31	21	128	24	147	19	171	20	193	25	155	22
Total	$ 147	100	$ 533	100	$786	100	$850	100	$ 758	100	$709	100

(Continued)

Table 42 (Continued)

	Year											
	1959 Value	%	1960 Value	%	1961 Value	%	1962 Value	%	1963 Value	%	1964 Value	%
Cotton[a]	198	26	157	20	160	19	218	23	196	20	169	16
Coffee	63	8	71	9	72	9	70	7	49	5	87	8
Sugar[b]	15	2	53	7	69	8	43	5	60	6	77	7
Meat[c]	48	6	43	5	58	7	74	8	63	6	42	4
Seafood	41	5	36	5	46	5	48	5	54	5	53	5
Copper[d]	30	4	26	3	19	2	24	3	22	2	14	1
Lead[e]	34	5	34	4	37	4	26	3	27	3	22	2
Zinc[f]	25	3	29	4	27	3	28	3	30	3	36	3
Sulfur	24	3	28	4	29	3	30	3	34	3	38	4
Petroleum[g]	27	4	20	3	33	4	38	4	37	4	38	4
Gold[h] and Silver	30	4	48	6	41	5	44	5	51	5	46	5
(12 products above)	535	(71)	545	(69)	591	(70)	643	(68)	623	(63)	622	(58)
All others	218	29	242	31	253	30	300	32	364	37	447	42
Total	$753	100	$787	100	$844	100	$943	100	$987	100	$1,069	100

Notes: All figures are rounded; -- indicates insignificant export values with percentage weights of less than 1 per cent; [a]raw cotton only; [b]raw and refined; [c]includes the value of live cattle and fresh or frozen carcasses as well; [d, e, f,] includes the value of ores, concentrates, and metals; [g]includes the value of crude petroleum and related products exported; [h]excludes monetary gold movements.

Sources: Same as Table 14, Chapter 3.

Table 43

Current Account Credits in the Mexican Balance of Payments, 1940-64
(In millions of U.S. dollars)

	1940	1945	1950	1951	1952	1953	1954	1955	1956
Merchandise Exports (f.o.b.)	85	266	483	577	618	559	616	738	807
Gold and Silver Exports	62	14	50	52	59	52	45	48	43
Migrant Workers' Remittances	---	55	19	30	29	34	28	25	38
Tourism	---	---	---	---	---	---	---	---	---
Border Trade[b]	---	---	---	---	---	---	---	---	---
(Tourism and Border Trade)[c]	(30)	(61)	(163)	(272)	(275)	(313)	(345)	(445)	(508)
Other	6	16	---	20	19	22	24	24	24
Totals									
(Old Series)[c]	(184)	(412)	(716)	(951)	(1,000)	(980)	(1,058)	(1,280)	(1,420)
New Series[b]									

(Continued)

Table 43 (Continued)

	1957	1958	1959	1960	1961	1962	1963[a]	1964[a]
Merchandise Exports (f.o.b.)	706	709	723	739	803	899	931	1,023
Gold and Silver Exports	52	49	30	48	41	44	51	45
Migrant Workers' Remittances	33	36	38	36	34	32	30	29
Tourism	---	134	142	155	164	179	210	241
Border Trade[b]	---	316	354	366	393	407	446	463
(Tourism and Border Trade)[c]	(592)	(542)	(636)	(670)	(724)	(822)	---	---
Other	24	24	30	28	28	26	35	35
Totals								
(Old Series)[c]	(1,406)	(1,361)	(1,457)	(1,520)	(1,630)	(1,823)	---	---
New Series[b]		1,268	1,317	1,372	1,463	1,587	1,703	1,811

Notes: Totals may not add due to rounding; --- indicates data not reported in sources; [a]preliminary data; [b]latest revised data; [c]old data series (see Appendix A above).

Sources: All data generated by: Banco de México, Departmento de Estudios Económicos, Division de Balanza de Pagos, reported in the following places: (1) Banco de México, Informe Anual, various issues; (2) Banco de Comercio Exterior, Comercio Exterior de México (Yearbook), various issues; (3) Report of the Combined Mexican Working Party, The Economic Development of Mexico (Baltimore: Johns Hopkins Press, 1953), pp. 348-361; (4) for the years of 1958-63, private communication to author, reporting revised data.

Table 44

Estimated Value of Mexico's Export and Import Coefficients, 1940-64
(Columns 3, 4, 5, 6, 7 are in millions of U.S. dollars)

	(1) GNP (millions of current pesos)	(2) Value of the Peso ($U.S. per peso)	(3) = (2)x(1) GNP	(4) Mdse. Export Earnings	(5) Total "Export" Earnings	(6) Mdse. Import Outlays	(7) Total "Import" Outlays	$(8)=\frac{(4)}{(3)}$	$(9)=\frac{(5)}{(3)}$	$(10)=\frac{(6)}{(3)}$	$(11)=\frac{(7)}{(3)}$
1940	7,300	.182	1,329	147	184	132	173	11.1	13.8	9.9	13.0
1945	20,500	.206	4,223	280	412	372	444	6.6	9.8	8.8	10.5
1950	40,577	.116	4,707	533	716	597	666	11.3	15.2	12.7	14.1
1955	87,349	.080	6,988	786	1,280	884	1,180	11.2	18.3	12.6	16.8
1960	154,137	.080	12,331	786	1,372	1,186	1,648	6.4	11.1	9.6	13.4
1961	163,757	.080	13,100	844	1,463	1,138	1,642	6.4	11.2	8.7	12.5
1962	177,533	.080	14,203	943	1,587	1,143	1,680	6.6	11.2	8.0	11.8
1963	192,200	.080	15,376	982	1,703	1,240	1,806	6.4	11.1	8.0	11.7
1964	211,500	.080	16,920	1,069	1,837	1,493	2,249	6.3	10.9	8.8	13.3

Notes: All figures in the $U.S. were converted at official average annual exchange rates. Data for 1964 are preliminary estimates. Export earnings include value of nonmonetary gold and silver exports. Note the caveats concerning reliability of balance of payments data discussed in Appendix A.

Sources: Same as Table 14, Chapter 3, and Table 39 of this Appendix.

Table 45

The Volume and Unit Values of Mexico's Registered Merchandise Trade, 1940-63 (1958=100)

Year	Quantum of Exports (1)	Quantum of Imports (2)	Unit Value of Exports (3)	Unit Value of Imports (4)	Terms of Trade (5)=(3)/(4)
1950	71	65	100	76	132
1955	99	85	108	92	117
1958	100	100	100	100	100
1960	106	98	98	107	92
1963	126	109	106	101	105

Notes: All indices based on U.S. dollar values of registered merchandise exports and imports at 1955 prices. The unit value indices are current year based (Paasche) type indices. For details, see the second source cited.

Sources: ECLA, *Statistical Bulletin for Latin America*, Vol. 1, No. 1, pp. 120-23, and Vol. II, No. 2, pp. 83-87.

Table 46

World Market Prices of Mexico's Principal Commodity Exports, 1939-64
(In U.S. cents per pound, unless noted otherwise)

Year	Cotton[a]	Raw Sugar[b]	Coffee[c]	Shrimp[d]	Lead[e]	Zinc[f]	Silver[g]	Copper[h]
1939-41[j]	13.7	3.1	11.6	----	5.2	6.3	36.2	11.4
1945	19.5	3.8	16.5	----	6.4	8.3	51.9	11.9
1950-52[j]	36.2	6.1	55.4	60.5	15.6	16.0	82.8	23.4
1955	24.4	6.0	60.1	60.5	14.9	12.3	89.1	37.4
1956	23.8	6.1	70.9	76.3	15.8	13.5	90.8	41.9
1957	24.7	6.2	60.9	89.2	14.5	11.4	90.8	30.0
1958	21.3	6.3	50.8	90.0	11.9	10.3	89.0	26.1
1959	23.6	6.2	43.2	74.4	12.0	11.5	91.2	30.8
1960	22.9	6.3	42.4	72.3	11.8	13.0	91.4	32.2
1961	22.8	6.3	39.3	77.5	10.7	11.5	92.4	30.2
1962	22.2	6.4	36.9	102.5	9.4	11.6	108.4	30.8
1963	23.2	8.2	36.5	90.1	10.9	12.0	127.9	30.8
1964	----	6.9	47.2	----	13.4	13.6	129.3	32.2

Notes:---- indicates data not reported in sources; [a]wholesale price, Torreon, Middling 15/16" fiber; [b]duty paid New York spot prices; [c]Coatepec, washed, duty paid spot prices at New York; [d]wholesale price, Chicago, 26-30 count, frozen and headless; [e]spot prices at St. Louis; [f]spot prices at St. Louis (prime slab zinc); [g]in U.S. cents per troy ounce, at N.Y., refined;[h] average spot price at N.Y., electrolytic copper; [j]average annual prices for the entire three years.

Sources: Cotton and shrimp data: FAO, Production Yearbook, various issues; all other prices: Commodity Research Bureau, Commodity Yearbook, various issues.

Table 47

The Direction of Mexico's Merchandise Trade, 1935-65
(Percentage Distribution)

	1935	1940	1945	1950	1955	1965
Registered Exports	100	100	100	100	100	100
The Americas	68.8	91.3	99.2	92.5	79.9	72.1
(U.S.A.)	(62.8)	(89.5)	(83.5)	(86.4)	(74.0)	(56.7)
(Others)	(6.0)	(1.8)	(15.7)	(6.2)	(5.9)	(15.4)
Europe	28.3	5.4	.5	5.5	13.8	15.2
Asia	1.9	3.0	---	1.7	5.9	9.9
Africa	---	---	---	---	.1	2.4
Oceania	.8	---	---	---	.2	.4
Registered Imports	100	100	100	100	100	100
The Americas	66.5	82.4	93.5	87.6	83.1	70.8
(U.S.A.)	(65.3)	(78.8)	(82.4)	(84.4)	(79.3)	(65.7)
(Others)	(1.2)	(3.6)	(11.1)	(3.2)	(3.8)	(5.1)
Europe	31.1	13.8	4.9	10.4	14.5	24.8
Asia	1.7	3.0	---	1.0	1.1	3.1
Africa	---	---	---	---	---	---
Oceania	---	.5	1.6	1.0	1.3	1.3

Note: Columns may not total due to rounding; --- indicates insignificant amounts.

Source: Banco Nacional de Comercio Exterior, Comercio Exterior de México (Yearbook), various issues.

Table 48

Value of All Crops Produced on Publicly Irrigated Land, by States, 1960-61
(In millions of pesos at market prices)

State	Distribution of Irrigated Crops		Distribution of Publicly Irrigated Land, by States, 1960-61
	Value	Per Cent	Per Cent
Baja California, (N. & S.)	975.3	16.9	41.1
Chihuahua	230.8	4.0	3.9
Coahuila, Durango, Nuevo Léon	628.3	10.9	13.7
Sinaloa	764.3	13.2	5.9
Sonora	1,329.2	23.0	20.1
Tamaulipas	546.3	9.5	17.3
Subtotal	4,474.2	77.5	75.0
All Other States	1,299.0	22.5	25.0
Total	5,773.2	100.0	100.0

Source: Same as Source No. 2, Table 50.

Table 49

Value of Seven Principal Crops Produced in 1960-61, by States
(Millions of pesos at market prices)

State	Cotton	Wheat	Rice	Tomatoes	Oranges	Corn	Cane Sugar
Baja California, N. & S.	529	106	---	4.2	1.1	5	.9
Coahuila	296	66	---	2.5	---	15	---
Chihuahua	313	51	---	1.8	1.2	154	.4
Durango	161	24	---	1.2	1.3	3	.8
Nuevo Léon	33	17	---	.8	157.8	65	.4
Sinaloa	222	5	122	122.5	2.3	102	91.3
Sonora	719	432	22	35.6	11.8	55	---
Tamaulipas	455	2	---	36.2	15.5	119	83.9
Subtotal	2,728	703	143	204.8	191.0	518	177.7
All Other States	120	330	149	88.9	290.9	3,408	785.1
Total	2,848	1,033	292	293.7	481.9	3,926	962.8
Per Cent of National Total Grown in Eight Northern States	95.8	68.1	49.0	69.7	39.6	13.2	18.5

Note: Baja California, South, is a Federal Territory and is included here with Baja California, North, a state; --- indicates insignificant values.

Source: Dirección General de Estadística, Anuario Estadístico, 1960-61 (Mexico: Talleres Gráficos Nacionales, 1963), pp. 352-64.

Table 50

Percentage of Major Crops Raised on Publicly Irrigated Land, by Value, 1960-61
(At market prices, in millions of pesos)

Crop	Value of Total Crop (1)	Value of Crops Grown in Irrigation Districts (2)	(2)/(1) Per Cent
Corn	3,925.8	511.1	13.0
Cotton	2,848.3	2,413.4	84.7
Wheat	1,033.2	893.5	86.5
Sugar Cane	962.8	317.9	33.0
Coffee	945.9	.7	---
Beans	709.0	147.3	20.8
Oranges	481.9	.3	---
Tomatoes	293.7	129.2	41.0
Subtotal	11,200.7	4,413.4	39.4
All other crops	5,198.0	1,359.8	26.2
Total	16,399.0	5,773.2	

Note: --- indicates insignificant amounts.

Sources: Column (1): Dirección General de Estadistica Anuario Estadístico, 1960-61 (México: Talleres Gráficos Nacionales, 1963), pp. 349-50.

Column (2): Secretaría de Recurcos Hidraulicos, Estadística Agricola, 1960-61 (México: Talleres Gráficos Nacionales, 1961), p. 247.

SELECTED BIBLIOGRAPHY

SELECTED BIBLIOGRAPHY

Books

Balassa, Bela A. Trade Prospects for Developing Countries. Homewood, Ill.: Richard D. Irwin, Inc., 1964.

Brandenburg, Frank. The Making of Modern Mexico. Englewood Cliffs, N.J.: Prentice-Hall, 1964.

Cline, Howard F. Mexico: Revolution to Evolution. New York: Oxford University Press, 1962.

Crowther, Geoffrey. Balances and Imbalances of Payments. Norwood, Mass.: The Plimpton Press, 1957.

Fei, John C.H., and Ranis, Gustav. Development of the Labor Surplus Economy. Homewood, Ill.: Richard D. Irwin, Inc., 1964.

Flores, Edmundo. Tratado de Economía Agrícola. Mexico: Fondo de Cultura Económica, 1961.

Fuente Rodriques José. El Deterio de la Relación de Intercambio y su Effecto en el Desarrollo Económico. Mexico: Universidad Nacional Autonoma de México. (Thesis), 1963.

Furtado, Celso. Development and Underdevelopment. Berkeley and Los Angeles: The University of California Press, 1964.

Glade, William P., and Anderson, Charles W. The Political Economy of Mexico. Madison: The University of Wisconsin Press, 1963.

Hirschman, Albert O. Latin American Issues, Essays and Comments. New York: The Twentieth Century Fund, 1961.

____. The Strategy of Economic Development. New Haven: Yale University Press, 1958.

Kindleberger, Charles P. Foreign Trade and the National Economy. New Haven: Yale University Press, 1962.

Meier, Gerald M. International Trade and Development. New York: Harper & Row, 1963.

____, (ed.). Leading Issues in Development Economics. New York: Oxford University Press, 1964.

Mosk, Sanford A. Industrial Revolution in Mexico. Berkeley: University of California Press, 1950.

Myrdal, Gunnar. The International Economy: Problems and Prospects. New York: Harper & Row, 1956.

Prebisch, Raul. The Economic Development of Latin America and Its Principal Problems. New York: United Nations, 1950.

Report of the Combined Mexican Working Party. The Economic Development of Mexico. Baltimore: The Johns Hopkins Press, 1953.

Rosas Figueroa, Aniceto, and Santillán Lopez, Roberto. Teoría General de las Finanzas Públicas y el Caso de México. México: Universidad Nacional Autonoma de México, 1962.

Ross, Stanford G., and Christensen, John B. Tax Incentives for Industry in Mexico. Cambridge: Harvard University Press, 1959.

United Nations. Commodity Trade and Economic Development. New York: United Nations, 1953.

____. International Compensation for Fluctuations in Commodity Trade. New York: United Nations, 1961.

Urquidi, Víctor L. Viabilidad económica de América Latina. Mexico: Fondo de Cultura Económica, 1962.

Vernon, Raymond. The Dilemma of Mexico's Development. Cambridge: Harvard University Press, 1963.

____, (ed.). Public Policy and Private Enterprise in Mexico. Cambridge: Harvard University Press, 1964.

Yáñez-Pérez, Luis. La Mecanización de la Agricultura Mexicana. Mexico: Editorial Cultura, 1957.

Yates, Paul Lamartine. El Desarrollo Regional de México. Mexico: Talleres Gráficos Victoria, 1962.

Articles, Periodicals, and Government Publications

Banco de México, S.A. Informe Anual (Annual Bulletin), 1950-66.

Banco Nacional de Comercio Exterior, S.A. Comercio Exterior de México (monthly edition in Spanish), 1950-66.

____. Comercio Exterior de México (Annual Yearbook), 1952-62.

____. Comercio Exterior de México (monthly edition in English), 1956-66.

____. Seis Años de Comercio Exterior. Mexico: Talleres Nacionales, 1965.

Banco Nacional de México, S.A. Review of the Economic Situation of Mexico (Monthly), 1950-66.

Bird, Richard. "The Economy of the Mexican Federal District," Inter-American Economic Affairs. Autumn, 1963.

Ellsworth, P.T. "The Terms of Trade Between Primary Producing and Industrial Countries," Inter-American Economic Affairs. Summer, 1956.

Fernandez y Fernandez, Ramón. "La reforma agraria mexicana: logros y problemas derivados," El Trimestre Económico. April-June, 1957.

Haberler, Gottfried. International Trade and Economic Development. Cairo: National Bank of Egypt, 1959.

Nacional Financiera, S.A. Informe Anual, various issues, 1958-65.

____. El Mercado de Valores (Weekly Bulletin), various issues, 1945-66.

Secretaría de Industria y Comercio, Dirección General de Estadística. Catologo General de las Estadísticas Nacionales. Mexico: Talleres Nacionales, 1960.

____. Anuario Estadístico, 1960-61. Mexico: Talleres Gráficos Nacionales, 1963.

____. Compendio Estadístoco. Mexico: Talleres Nacionales, various issues.

Sturmthal, Adolf. "Economic Development, Income Distribution and Capital Formation in Mexico," The Journal of Political Economy, June, 1955.

U.S. Bureau of Foreign Commerce. Investment in Mexico. Washington, D.C.: U.S. Government Printing Office, 1957.

U.S. Department of Labor, Bureau of Labor Statistics. Labor in Mexico (B.L.S. Report No. 251). Washington, D.C.: U.S. Government Printing Office, 1962.

Wionczek, Miguel S. "Los excedentes mundiales y la politica agrícola exterior de los Estados Unidos," El Trimestre Económico. September-December, 1954.

ABOUT THE AUTHOR

William O. Freithaler is Assistant Professor of Economics at the University of Virginia and is currently engaged in research into the problems of underdeveloped countries. In 1966, he received his Ph.D. degree at the University of Michigan, where he served as instructor in the Department of Economics. He has also studied at the University of Texas and the University of California at Berkeley.

As a Foreign Area Fellow, Dr. Freithaler devoted 1964-65 to studies of noneconomic aspects of Latin American culture. He has traveled and worked in Colombia, Mexico, and Peru.